LIVING THE WORD

A DEVOTIONAL AND PRACTICAL
COMMENTARY ON PSALM 119

BY
KELSEY GARMAN

DISCOVERING THE POWER OF GOD'S WORD
IN THE BELIEVER'S LIFE

Xulon
PRESS

DEDICATION

TO
My wife, Joyce,
whose assistance and suggestions
have made this a better book.

Set your hearts on all the words which I testify among you today, which you shall command your children to be careful to observe, all the words of this law. For it is not a little thing for you, because it is your life.
                                              —Deuteronomy 32:46-47

It is the Spirit who gives life, the flesh profits nothing. The words that I speak to you, they are spirit and they are life.
                                              —John 6:63

For the word of God is living and powerful, and sharper than any two-edged sword, piercing even to the division of soul and spirit, and of joints and marrow, and is a discerner of the thoughts and intents of the heart.
                                              —Hebrews 4:12

CONTENTS

PREFACE

Many writers, past and present, have loved Psalm 119 and written of its riches. So why should I add my name to their number? I make no claim to superior scholarship or better writing skills than others, but I do have a different perspective on this unique treasure from God's Word.

Because great preachers have preached from a particular text doesn't mean that men with lesser knowledge or gifts shouldn't preach from it. Each preacher and writer brings to the exposition of God's Word something of himself, something no one else can bring.

This psalm became especially precious to me a few years ago when double trouble descended upon my peaceful life. While I was undergoing treatment for prostate cancer, some serious accusations were made against me by a government agency. During that trying time I learned to cling to the Word of God as never before, especially to Psalm 119. By God's grace I survived both trials with a deeper loved for God and His Word.

There's no greater need in the church today than for a return to belief in the authority of God's everlasting Word which is "profitable for doctrine, for reproof, for correction and instruction in righteousness" (II Tim. 3:16). I believe the greatest contribution I can make to the body of Christ is to lift up the eternal truth of God's Word as it's presented in Psalm 119. If I can do only one thing, in whatever time God may give me, let this be it. And to Him be the glory!

This book isn't a theological book. It's a devotional and practical commentary written to help the reader capture the psalmist's love for God's Word and make it his own in all circumstances of life. I hope it will also provide an analytical framework to help preachers and teachers present it to their congregations and classes.

Since it isn't a theological book, it isn't written in theological jargon. It's written in the conversational style I've used during my many years of writing for newspapers and magazines.

I have used alliterative outlines for each stanza for two reasons. They help me to analyze the text, and they provide a handy outline for preaching and teaching. I have also written a four-line poem paraphrasing each verse. I don't claim that these little verses are good poetry. In fact, some of them are rather bad, but they were written as the result of my own meditation on each verse. I suggest you write your own verses as you study the psalm. Your poetry will probably be much better than mine.

I have read nearly all the books currently available on Psalm 119 and have gleaned something from each of them. If I have I have used materials from any publications without giving due credit, it is not intentional. I have quoted extensively from "The Golden Alphabet," by Charles Spurgeon, published by Pilgrim Publications, Pasadena, TX. Other helpful works are; "The Word of God in the Child of God," by George J. Zemek, a privately published book, Mango, FL. and "Exploring the Psalms Volume 2," by John Phillips published by Loizeaux Brothers, Neptune, N J. Dr. Phillips' outlines were particularly helpful. Many of my outlines are derived in part from his. All quotes from these authors are from these works unless otherwise indicated.

If you want to derive the greatest benefit from the study of this psalm, I suggest that you **1. Read it repeatedly.** You might read one stanza daily for a week, then move on to another one the next week. Using this approach you can go through the psalm twice a year and have eight weeks left over.

Spurgeon said, "Its variety is that of a kaleidoscope. In the kaleidoscope you look once and there is a strangely beautiful form. You shift the glass a little and another shape, equally beautiful, appears...The more one studies it the fresher it becomes. The more you look at it the more you will see in it."

2. Meditate on it continually. Studying the psalm will get it into your head, but meditating on it will get it into your life. Seven times in the psalm the psalmist speaks of his own meditation on the Word of God. According to Spurgeon, Matthew Henry's father, Phillip, advised his children to take one verse a day of Psalm 119 and meditate on it, and so go through its 176 verses twice each year. Matthew Henry came to love it and later became a great Bible expositor.

3. Memorize it faithfully. Memorizing the entire 119th Psalm may seem like a daunting task to most of us. Yet many have done it. William Wilberforce, the British politician who almost single-handedly put an end to the slave trade in England, memorized it and often quoted from it. Both Henry Martyn, famous missionary to India, and David Livingstone, perhaps the most famous of all missionaries to Africa, memorized it.

Maybe you've already memorized some of its key verses. As you study it and meditate on it, store other verses in your memory. It will enrich your life.

4. Apply it personally. It would be tragic if you studied it, meditated on it and memorized it, without it producing any change in your life. The psalmist places repeated emphasis on obeying the Word. The Pharisees of Jesus' day could quote vast portions of Scripture, but didn't obey them. Change can only come as we obey.

Psalm 119 is the psalmist's prayer journal where he records the longings of his heart for God and His Word. If we make it our passionate prayer our lives will change forever.

Spurgeon said of it, "It is an incense made up of many spices, but they are wonderfully blended together to form one sweetness."

May you find it so as you explore this wonderful treasure!

INTRODUCTION

Psalm 119 has 176 verses arranged in 22 stanzas, or strophes, of eight verses each. One stanza is assigned to each letter of the Hebrew alphabet, and each verse in that stanza starts with the letter assigned to it. For example, all the verses in the first stanza start with the letter "aleph," the first letter of the Hebrew alphabet.

This is known as an acrostic poem, found often in ancient poetry. However, the only other extended use of it in the Bible is the book of Lamentations. Perhaps the psalmist used the acrostic to make the psalm easier to memorize. Another possible reason was to convey the idea that he was covering his subject completely. It's like our saying we cover some subject from A to Z. He is saying he is covering the Word of God from Aleph to Taw.

Some critics have said the acrostic structure of the psalm detracts from its content. One says its repetitions are tedious and it exhibits poor thought sequence. Another describes it as a mosaic of thoughts which are repeated in a wearisome manner.

But Spurgeon said, "Its expressions are as many as the waves, but the testimony is one as the sea." And, "It runs up and down the same scale but every song is different." And Alexander McClaren said, "There is music in the monotony."

The theme of Psalm 119 is the Word of God, and the writer uses eight Hebrew synonyms to describe the different aspects of the Word he wants to convey. The first is *torah,* which appears 29 times and is translated "law." In its narrow sense it refers to the Mosaic Law. In its broader sense it's used to describe the Scriptures as a whole in which God communicates His will and purpose to man.

The second word is *edut,* used 23 times and translated "testimonies." It relates to bearing witness to the truth. It implies that God's Word is His affirmation to the truth. In Deuteronomy 31:26, God told Israel to place the book of the law beside the Ark of the Covenant "that it may be there as a witness against you."

The third synonym is *piqqudim,* which appears 21 times and is translated "precepts." It has the idea of something fixed or appointed such as a boundary. It can also mean the fixed orders which come from a master to a servant.

The next word is *huqqa.* It occurs 22 times and is translated "statutes." It comes from a word which means to hew, cut or engrave. Statutes are the permanently engraved mandates which God has given us to obey.

The fifth synonym is *miswa,* translated "commandments." Used 21 times, it emphasizes the authority of what is said. God's commandments are not the suggestions of a friend. They are the orders of the supreme sovereign of the universe.

The next word is *mispat,* used 23 times and translated "judgments." It refers to legal decisions handed down by a judge in a court of law, or by a ruler settling a dispute among his subjects. The Bible is a record of God's infallible judgments, either declared or demonstrated, in the affairs of His people.

Another word is *dabar,* translated "word" about 400 times in the Old Testament and 24 times in this psalm. It's the general term for God's communication of His will and purpose to man. It's the word that proceeds from the mouth of God.

The eighth and final word is *imra.* It appears 19 times and is also translated "word," but conveys the idea of promise.

Each of these words has a slightly different shade of meaning, but all are God's Word and I will speak of them as such in my comments. Derek Kidner, in his commentary on the Psalms, gives us a picture of how we should strike a balance between these eight words in the psalm.

> Like a ring of eight bells, eight synonyms for Scripture dominate the psalm and 22 stanzas will ring the changes on them…The synonyms belong together and we should probably not look for each to show its distinct character at each occurrence, but rather to contribute, by its frequent arrival, to our total understanding of what Scripture is.

Like its author, the Word of God is shown in Psalm 119 to be righteous, faithful and perfect. In it we find an unchanging standard of truth and righteousness for every circumstance of life.

The author and date of the psalm is unknown. Jewish tradition says it was written during the Babylonian exile by Ezra, but there is no evidence to support it. Christians have generally believed it was penned by David, but again, the evidence to support it is lacking. It's true that some passages could parallel David's experiences, but they could also relate to the experiences of many others.

I'm inclined to believe it was written during the exile by Daniel. It parallels Daniel's experiences even more than those of David. He cleansed his way by obeying God's law as a youth (v.9). He was a stranger and a pilgrim in a foreign land (vs. 19, 54). He was reproached, derided and slandered (vs. 22,23,51,69), and princes plotted against him (vs. 78, 85,86,95,110,161). Yet he spoke of God's testimonies before kings (v.46). The whole psalm reflects the life of one who was disciplined by the law from an early age, but whose life was marked by many trials. That certainly describes Daniel.

However, since we don't know who the author is I will refer to him only as the psalmist. It's not necessary for us to know when it was written, or by whom. It's enough to know it was inspired by the Holy Spirit and its truths are as valuable today as when they were first written.

The central truth of Psalm 119 is that a commitment to obeying God's Word is necessary to a life pleasing to God, and that such obedience is impossible without God's help.

This psalm wasn't written in an ivory tower. The psalmist was acquainted with the struggles that come from living for God in a hostile world. He was pursued and oppressed by evil men who set traps for him. He experienced discouragement, sorrow and depression. Yet he constantly cried out to God and found solace in His Word.

So can you!

STANZA 1: PSALM 119:1-8

THE SECRET OF HAPPINESS

I. The Description of a Happy Man vs. 1-3
   A. His Character vs.1-2
      1. His purity v.1
      2. His principles v.2
   B. His Conduct v.3
II. The Dilemma of a Helpless Man vs. 4-6
   A. The Prescription for Happiness v.4
   B. The Prayer for Help vs. 5-6
      1. In acquiring direction v.5
      2. In avoiding disgrace v.6
III. The Decisions of a Hopeful Man vs. 7-8
   A. To Praise God's Ways v. 7
   B. To Practice God's Word v. 8

This stanza introduces the psalm by clearly pointing out that happiness is found by obeying

God's Word. The psalmist declares it as a principle in verses 1-3 by speaking in the third person. As the stanza progresses he applies the principle to himself by changing to the first person

I. THE DESCRIPTION OF A HAPPY MAN
VS.1-3

A. His Character vs.1-2
 1. His purity v.1

Blessed are the undefiled in the way who walk in the law of the Lord. The Hebrew word *esher,* translated "blessed" here, is in the plural and means multiple blessings. The idea is that of many blessings, much happiness or good fortune. But it's not the happiness or good fortune that comes from what happens to us, but rather from God's favor. It has no connection to the circumstances of life. As the entire psalm shows, this blessedness comes from seeking God and obeying His Word with all our hearts. Real happiness comes from holy living and is unrelated to the pleasure, position, power, popularity or prosperity the world offers.

The word translated "undefiled" was originally a term which described those who had not touched a dead body or other unclean thing. However, the prophets spoke of those who were legally undefiled, but were spiritually and morally defiled because of their evil hearts. In the New Testament, the Pharisees thought themselves undefiled if they avoided legal defilement even though they committed acts of moral defilement. Jesus condemned them saying that the things which defile man are things that come from the heart.

So defilement is a condition of the heart. To be undefiled is to have a clean heart and a clear conscience toward God. It isn't just observing outward rituals. We're made clean through the blood of Jesus, yet we have to live in an evil world. Jesus prayed, "I pray not that You would take them out of the world, but that You would keep them from evil" (John 17:13-15).

As we walk through the filth of the world we will become defiled by it unless we're cleansed daily and sanctified. Jesus also prayed to the Father, "Sanctify them through Your truth, Your Word is truth" (John 17:17). That's why we must live in the Word every day.

To be undefiled is to live with an undivided and unpolluted heart. Joseph lived an undefiled life as did Daniel. David's life was marked by sin, but he repeatedly cried out to God for forgiveness and cleansing.

The undefiled walk according to the guidance found in the law. Their minds are fixed on it. They don't walk in the counsel of the ungodly, stand in the way of the sinful or sit in the seat of the scornful. Rather, they meditate on the law day and night (Ps.1:1-2).

The word law should be understood today in its wider sense as all the revealed Word of God. Happy, happy is the person who purifies his life and lives by the principles revealed in it. May our prayer be, "Search me O God and know my heart, try me and see if there be any wicked way in me, and lead me in the way everlasting" (Ps. 138:23-24).

O Lord, let me be pure
In all the things I say,
And let my walk be sure
Every hour of every day.

2. His priorities v.2

Blessed are they who keep His testimonies; that seek Him with the whole heart. The New Century Version says, "Happy are those who keep His rules and try to obey them with the whole heart." The Message paraphrase says, "You are blessed when you follow His directions, doing your best to find Him."

These translations suggest that we find Him by keeping His testimonies. So the seekers and the keepers are the same, and keeping and seeking is the same thing. It's in keeping His testimonies with the whole heart that we find Him.

The word "keep" is *natsar.* It means to guard as to guard a city or to guard prisoners. It can also mean to watch, obey or faithfully perform something. It's often used to describe keeping covenant. God keeps covenant with Israel (Deut. 7:9), and Israel with God (Deut. 33:9). In Psalm 25:10, covenant and testimonies are equated. In this verse "keep" is used in the sense of faithfully obeying God's testimonies. Those who do so wholeheartedly are blessed. Jesus confirmed this when He said, "Blessed are those who hear the Word of God and keep it" (Luke 11:28).

Those who love the book want to know the author. God blesses only those who want to know Him and seek Him with the whole heart. Jesus told us to seek first the kingdom of God and His righteousness (Matt. 6:33), and to love the Lord with all our hearts (Matt. 22:37-38). A 15-minute daily "quiet time" hardly qualifies as seeking Him with the whole heart.

Certain kings of Judah and Israel are said to have followed the Lord in some things but not in others. In most cases, where they didn't completely follow the Lord, they worshipped the Lord, but allowed idols to be worshipped in the land. In a similar way, the degree that we follow the Lord may be measured by what we allow in our lives.

Paul demonstrated that he followed the Lord with his whole heart when he said, "This one thing I do... I press toward the goal for the prize of the upward call of God in Christ Jesus" (Phil. 3:14).

By keeping Thy Word I am blessed,
So with my whole heart I obey,
And make to Thee this request,
That I might walk with Thee today.

B. His Conduct v.3

They also do no iniquity. They walk in His ways. The "they" here are the seekers and keepers of verse 2. In addition to seeking the Lord and keeping His testimonies wholeheartedly, they do no iniquity. Being undefiled has to do with the condition of our hearts. Iniquity has to do with our behavior toward others. It means to be unjust, dishonest, devious, tricky, twisted or perverse. The Spurrell translation of the Old Testament says, "They shall not commit deeds of oppression." R.K. Harrison's translation says, "They commit no injustices." So iniquity is the opposite of fairness and honesty. Those who do no iniquity are blameless in the sight of others.

Our journey through life should reflect God's ways. To the extent that we keep His testimonies and wholeheartedly seek Him, we will walk in His ways. The truly blessed man is one who is undefiled in his character and upright in his conduct. It's not enough to believe the truth we must walk in it.

With a heart that is upright
I seek my ways to mend,
To be pleasing in Thy sight,
And others not to offend.

II. THE DILEMMA OF A HOPELESS MAN VS. 4-6

A. The Prescription for Happiness v. 4

You have commanded us to keep Your precepts diligently. The Lord COMMANDED us to keep His precepts. It's not a suggestion. It's a directive from the God of the universe. The word "keep" isn't the same word used in verse 2, but it has the same meaning. It's used in the active sense here. We're not just to hold on to his precepts in order to preserve them; we are to actively pursue them.

26

Diligently means greatly, mightily, exceedingly or beyond the ordinary. If we are to be happy and blessed, keeping the Lord's precepts must go beyond just a causal observance. Diligently here corresponds to "with the whole heart" in verse 2. We must aggressively obey His commands to preach the gospel, to witness, to meet the needs of the poor and do good works. We're to seek out opportunities rather than waiting for them to come to us. Paul tells us to "be zealous of good works" (Titus 2:14).

The person who hears what God says and doesn't obey Him is like the foolish man who builds his house on the sand only to see it swept away in the flood (Matt. 7:26-27).

> Thy word to us has been
> To keep Thy precepts with zeal,
> To avoid the ways of sin,
> And no wrong to conceal.

B. The Prayer for Help vs. 5-6
  1. In acquiring direction v.5
O that my ways were directed to keep Your statutes. The psalmist understands the requirements for a happy life – to be undefiled, to seek God with his whole heart, to do no iniquity. Yet he knows he can't do it. So he cries out for God's help. His prayer is expressed as a deep longing; O that it might be so!

It's not his desire that needs direction, but his ways. He has the desire to do what is needed but he lacks the ability. Like Paul, he delighted in the law after the inward man, but another law worked in him warring against that inward law so what he willed to do, he couldn't do (Rom 7). His dilemma is that he has the obligation and the desire to obey, but not the ability.

His plea is for God to direct his ways. The psalmist often uses the Hebrew word *kun* translated "directed" here. Its basic meaning is to fix, to prepare or make ready. We will see it several times later in the psalm with different shades of meaning.

He realizes that only God can make his ways consistent with his desires. We too must cry out with the psalmist and with Jeremiah, "Turn me and I will be turned" (Jer. 31:18). When God commands us to do something we can be assured that He will give us the ability to do it. Jesus said, "Without Me you can do nothing" (John 15:5). Every human weakness is an opportunity for God to show His strength.

> O Lord, my ways direct
> To the statutes Thou hast given,
> And let my life reflect
> That my sins are forgiven.

2. In avoiding disgrace v.6

Then I would not be ashamed when I look into all Your commandments. Sin brings shame. Adam and Eve were naked and unashamed until sin drove them into hiding. Defilement and iniquity bring shame, humiliation and disgrace. To suffer shame was the ultimate tragedy in the ancient Middle East.

Shame takes two forms. It may be a public disgrace as a result of some outward moral failure.

Or, it could be pangs of conscience for private sins. This is what the psalmist seems to fear most. We feel shame until sin is taken away by Christ. We can't keep the law, but Christ kept it for us. He took away our sin and endured our shame.

The psalmist prayed to avoid shame by looking into God's commandments. The word translated "look into" is a Hebrew word that means to focus on and follow carefully with the eye. It's used to describe an eagle eying its prey from high in the sky. Note that ALL of God's commandments are to be followed, not just the easy ones. We are not to compromise in keeping even the smallest commandment. They are all important. The Lord told Joshua to observe and do ALL the things that are written in the law (Josh. 1:7-8). Daniel could have compromised on what he ate and where or when he prayed, but he didn't.

God commanded King Saul to slay all the Amalakites. However, he left one alive and it brought him shame and rejection. One secret sin can rob us of God's blessing and steal our happiness. One compromise can bring us into bondage. There are many commandments, but only one law, and breaking one commandment makes us guilty of breaking the law, and guilt brings shame.

Shame is almost nonexistent in our culture. Sins once driven into the closet by shame are now proudly flaunted in the movies and the media. Deeds once done in the darkness are now boldly done in the day with the approval of a decadent society. But there will be a day when the wicked will appear before God in judgment and will hide their faces in shame.

I will never be ashamed
When I look into Thy Word,
So let no other name be named,
And no other voice be heard.

And Isaac Watts wrote:

Then shall my heart have inward joy
And keep my face from shame
When all Thy statutes I obey
And honor all Thy name.

III. THE DECISIONS Of A HOPEFUL MAN VS. 7-8

A. To Praise God's Ways v.7
I will praise You with uprightness of heart when I learn Your righteous judgments. Defilement and iniquity lead to shame. Seeking the Lord and obeying His Word leads to praise. Uprightness means to be straight, honest and sincere. Only honest and sincere praise is real. Second hand praise is not pleasing to God.

The Bible is a record, not only of what God has declared to be right, but of what He has done – things that show His judgments are right. The more study His Word the more we learn about the rightness of His words and His ways. The more we learn of Him the more we praise Him. As we study His Word and obey it, we see His righteous judgments playing out in our lives, and that what He does is always right for us.

I will crown Thy name with praise
From a heart that is honest and true,
When I learn of Thy ways,
I will give Thee the honor due.

B. To Practice God's Word v.8

I will keep Your statutes; Oh do not forsake me utterly. It's not enough to learn God's statutes; we must obey them. As we study the Bible we must adjust our ways to conform to its unchanging decrees. Today, some are reinterpreting the Bible to make it compatible with our modern culture. But God's Word doesn't change. If it declared something to be true 3,000 years ago, it's still true today.

The phrase "do not forsake me utterly" seems to be a prelude to the trials which the psalmist will endure in the verses ahead. The word "utterly" is the same word translated "diligently" in verse 4, meaning exceedingly or beyond the ordinary. No matter what trials we face, we have the promise "I will never leave you or forsake you" (Heb. 13:5). The Living Bible paraphrases it, "Please, don't give up on me."

Thy statutes I long to obey.
It is my heart's desire,
So forsake me not I pray,
But give me the grace I require.

THE PATHWAY TO PURITY

I.   He Reveals the Principle of Purity v.9
II. He Reviews the Pathway to Purity vs.10-14
   A. What He Did vs.10-12
      1. He sought God v.10
      2. He stored up God's Word v.11
      3. He searched for God's wisdom v.12
      4. He spoke God's Word v.13
   B. What He Discovered v.14
III. He Resolves to Pursue Purity vs. 15-16
   A. He Resolved to Ruminate on God's Word v.15a
   B. He Resolved to Reflect on God's Ways v.15b
   C. He Resolved to Rejoice in God's Word v.16a
   D. He Resolved to Remember God's Word v.16b

In the first stanza the psalmist speaks of the blessedness of those who are undefiled and do no iniquity. In this stanza he gives us the secret of blameless living and leads us down the pathway of purity. God will make us clean if we are willing to commit our lives to walk according to His Word.

I. HE REVEALS THE PRINCIPLE OF PURITY V.9

How can a young man cleanse his way? By taking heed according to Your word. The best way to live pure life is to start early. It's much easier to live in purity throughout life if we start when we are young. That's why Paul told Timothy to flee youthful lusts. (II Tim. 2:22)

Youth is a time of special danger because of youth's natural lack of restraint. When we're young we don't have the experience to make us cautious, so we're prone to the unrestrained pursue of our passions. A youth minister recently told me the young people he was ministering to thought they were invincible. "They define a good time only in terms of instant gratification," he said.

The young man or woman who adopts the Bible as a guide and teacher is indeed fortunate. Youth is the time to wholeheartedly seek God and obey His Word. Solomon said, "Remember your creator in the days of your youth before the difficult days come and the years where you say, 'I have no pleasure in them'" (Eccl. 12:1).

None of us can say we've made ourselves pure. "Who can say, 'I have made my heart clean, I am pure from my sins'" (Prov. 20:9)? There's only one standard of purity and that's God's standard as revealed in the Bible. Our standards are meaningless. We can live pure lives only by measuring ourselves by the Word of God.

The Word of God cleanses us because it is pure. "The commandments of the Lord are pure, enlightening the eyes" (Ps.19:8). "The words of the Lord are pure words" (Ps.12:6). "Every word of God is pure" (Prov. 30:5). Jesus told the apostles, "You are already clean through the word I have spoken to you" (John 15:3). Later, Paul wrote, "That He (Christ) might sanctify and cleanse it (the church) with the washing of water by the word" (Eph. 5:26).

The principle of purity is clear. We must make God's Word their standard of conduct. We must not compromise our conduct to conform to what we hear, see or read, if it is contrary to the standards of God's Word.

How can I make my heart pure
While still in the bloom of my youth?
How can I make my way sure?
By giving heed to Thy words of truth!

II. HE REVIEWS THE PATHWAY TO
PURITY VS.10-14

A. What He Did vs.10-12

The following five verses tell us what the psalmist has already done, as he walked along the pathway of purity. Four times in these verses he says."I have…"

1. He sought God v.10

With my whole heart I have sought You. O let me not wander from Your commandments. He said in verse 2, that a whole hearted commitment was necessary for a blessed life. Here, he makes that commitment. A wholehearted commitment to seek God is the first step on the pathway of a pure life.

Living a pure life isn't a casual business, or a halfhearted pursuit. There are no casual musicians playing in great orchestras, and no halfhearted athletes performing in the Olympics. There are no halfhearted Christians among the holy and the happy.

The psalmist had fixed his heart upon God, but he was afraid he might wander from obedience to His commandments. The word translated "wander" means to stray. It's used to describe a straying sheep (Isa. 53:6). Here it's passive, meaning to be led astray. In this form, it usually describes unintended straying rather than rebellion. Only the Lord can keep us from straying. If left to ourselves we'll wander away like foolish sheep. A rambling thought or a wandering look may lead us outside the boundaries of His statutes. Unless we are wholehearted seekers, we will be halfhearted wanderers.

The more wholeheartedly we seek Him the more sensitive we become to our proneness to wander, and the more we feel the need for prayer. Hymn writer Robert Robinson expressed it this way:

Let Thy grace like a fetter
Bind my wandering heart to Thee
Prone to wander, Lord I feel it
Prone to leave the God I love.
Here's my heart, O take and seal it,
Seal it for Thy courts above.

Some may argue that the psalmist lived under the law, but under grace we don't need such strict obedience to God's commandments. Grace is no excuse for lax living. Grace doesn't give us permission to sin; it gives us the power to be holy.

Even a small drifting can have great consequences. A ship once drifted several hundred miles off course. The captain discovered a small nail in the wall near the compass that caused the compass to be off by one degree. A small matter, but, over time, it caused a major deviation in the ship's course. The Bible is a perfect compass for life, but if we yield to even the smallest worldly influences in our lives we will wander off course, sometimes with disastrous consequences.

My heart is set on Thy face,
And I ponder all that You say.
I pray each day for Thy grace
That I may not wander away.

2. He stored up God's Word v.11

Your word I have hidden in my heart that I might not sin against You. In verse 3, the psalmist speaks of doing no iniquity. In this verse, he tells us the way to avoid it is by hiding God's Word in our hearts. We think he was speaking of memorizing it, and he probably was. But hiding the Word in our hearts goes beyond rote memory. A person may memorize vast portions of Scripture and still live a sinful life. The word "hide" is used in two ways. It may mean hiding something of great value, such as a treasure. It can also mean to store up for future use. Both applications are appropriate here. Some translations say, "I have treasured Your word in my heart."

The psalmist treasured it up in his heart as a shield against temptation. God's Word is not to be carried on a charm bracelet or put on a bumper sticker. It's stored in the heart. The battle for purity is fought in the heart. Solomon said, "Keep the heart with all diligence for out of it spring the issues of life" (Prov.4:23). The heart must be fortified with God's Word. Study gets us into the Word. Hiding it in our hearts gets it into us.

The Word keeps us from sinning against God. All sin is against God and God alone. Joseph, when tempted by Potiphar's wife, said, "How can I do this great wickedness and sin against God" (Gen. 39:9)? After his sin with Bathsheba and the murder of her husband, David prayed to God, "Against You, and You only, have I sinned" (Ps.51:4). Upon his return home the prodigal son said to his father, "I have sinned against heaven and in your sight" (Luke 15:21).

Treasuring God's Word in His heart enabled Jesus to resist the devil's temptations three times by quoting the Scriptures. Satan can't stand against God's Word. John said, "I have written to you young men because you are strong and the word of God abides in you and you have overcome the wicked one" (I John 2:14). Satan promises to give us everything we want but in reality, he wants to take away everything we have. The Word in the heart guards our steps. "The law of God is in his heart and none of his steps shall slide" (Ps. 37:31).

One preacher's outline of this verse is:

1. The best thing – Your word
2. The best place – In my heart
3. The best purpose – That I might not sin against You

And

In my heart Thy Word I've treasured.
It is with me every hour.
It brings me joy unmeasured
And keeps me from sin's dread power.

3. He searched for God's wisdom v.12

Blessed are You O Lord! Teach me Your statutes. In verse 7 the psalmist promised to praise God when he learned of His righteous judgments. Now he praises Him and prays to learn more.

We frequently find expressions of praise to the Lord in the Old Testament, especially in the psalms.

Praise is the natural expression of a pure heart. It's usually, but not always, offered in connection with an acknowledgement of the Lord's benefits to His people. In Psalm 102 we read, "Bless the Lord O my soul, and all that is within me. Bless His holy name. Bless the Lord O my soul and forget not all His benefits." The psalm then goes on to name His benefits to Israel.

In Revelation 15, John saw the saints, who had overcome the beast, singing praises to God. They sang the song of Moses and of the Lamb saying, "Great and marvelous are your works, Lord God Almighty. Just and true are your ways, O King of the saints" (verse.3). Perhaps the highest expression of praise in the New Testament is found in Ephesians 1:3 where Paul says, "Blessed be the God and Father of our Lord Jesus Christ, who has blessed us with all spiritual blessings in heavenly places in Christ Jesus."

The word "blessed" used in verse 12 is not the same word translated blessed in verses 1 and 2. The word here is *barak* which means to bend the knee, to praise or salute. The idea of kneeling before Him suggests recognition of who He is and what He has done. Perhaps the psalmist interjects his praise here as he contemplates the wonders of God's Word and its power to keep from sin.

When men teach, we may gain knowledge, but we learn holiness only from God. The psalmist is seeking purity of heart, not just learning, so he sat at the feet of the teacher of holiness.

"Teach me" is a prayer the psalmist repeats often. He had an unquenchable hunger to learn more about God and His Word. It's a request that we too should make every day.

> Lord, I bless Thy holy name!
> Teach me now Thy Word
> That ever remains the same,
> Yet new each time it's heard.

4. He spoke God's Word v.13

With my lips I have declared all the judgments of Your mouth. The word "declared" comes from *sapar,* which means to relate important information. It's not enough for God's Word to be hidden in our hearts, we must declare or confess it before men. To declare or confess God's Word implies that we fully agree with all His judgments. It's our "amen." It also establishes the truth of what He has said firmly in our hearts. "You shall declare a thing and it will be established for you" (Job 22:28).

When God's Word burns within us it can't be contained. Jeremiah said, "...His Word was like a burning fire shut up in my bones. I was weary of holding it back and I could not" (Jer. 20:19). The words we have learned in secret must be proclaimed in public. Jesus said, Whatever I tell you in the dark, speak in the light, and whatever you hear in the ear, preach on the housetops"(Matt. 10:27). So the necessity of declaring the Word of God is both compelled from within and commanded by God. If we don't declare it, many will never hear it.

We must be sure that what comes out of our mouths is what we have received from God's Word. Let us teach others only what God has taught us. The psalmist had declared ALL of God's judgments, not just the ones he thought people wanted to hear. He didn't just tell them how they could be more successful on the job, how to have a happy marriage, or how to be healthy and wealthy. In Psalm 71:15 we read, "My mouth shall tell of Your righteousness and Your salvation all the day." May it be so with us!

The declared word is a weapon and a shield against sin. It's the sword of the Spirit in our battle against evil (Eph. 6:17). In Revelation 12:11 we read of the brethren who overcame the devil "by the blood of the Lamb and the word of their testimony." It's the spoken word, not the secret word, that becomes a force for good on earth, but it must be heard in secret for it to have power when spoken publicly.

> All Thy words I have believed,
> And stored them in my heart.
> I now declare all I have received
> To others Thy truth to impart.

B. What He Discovered. v.14

I have rejoiced in the way of Your testimonies, as much as in all riches. As noted earlier God's testimonies refer to His witness to what He has done. The 10 Commandments are called a testimony. The Ark of the Covenant and the Tabernacle are called testimonies (Ex.22:16,38:21,25:32). Later the whole body of Scripture was considered God's testimony, or witness, of what He had done.

While he may have found joy in God's testimonies themselves, that's not what the psalmist is saying here. His joy was not in just studying God's Word and treasuring it up in his heart. Rather it was found in the WAY of God's testimonies. It was in the way they opened up to him – the way of purity and blessing. When we make a wholehearted commitment to obey the Word of God it gives us the power to live in a way that's contrary to our sinful natures. It's the pathway to purity and holy living. It's the way that Isaiah called, "the highway of holiness" (Isa.35:8). Jeremiah told Israel to "ask for the old paths where the good way is, and walk in it, then you will find rest for your souls" (Jer. 6:16).

A casual reading of verse 14 may lead us to believe that the psalmist found the way of God's testimonies and earthly wealth as equal reasons for rejoicing. However, the "as much as" is not in the original, but was supplied by the translators, as the italics in the King James Version and some other versions, indicate. It's clear from verses 72 and 127 that he treasured God's Word above all earthly wealth.

Men rejoice in worldly wealth because they think it will enable them to broaden their lives, and increase their pleasures and happiness. But all too often this broad road paved with riches leads to unhappiness and finally to destruction. The way of God's testimonies is narrow, but it's the way of real joy, the way of eternal life though Jesus Christ, who is the way, the truth and the life. There is far more real happiness on the pathway to purity than on the road to riches.

> Thy Word is my greatest possession,
> My earthly wealth it exceeds.
> It is the purest expression
> Of the joy that from Thee proceeds.

III. HE RESOLVES TO PURSUE PURITY
VS.15-16

A. He Resolved to Ruminate on God's Word v.15a

I will meditate on Your precepts. The Hebrew word for meditate used here means to ponder, muse, ruminate, mutter or to talk to oneself. The basic idea is to turn something over and over in the mind. The psalmist uses it eight times in Psalm 119. We all meditate on something. Sometimes we meditate on what we are afraid might happen. That's called worry. At other times, we meditate on things we enjoy, or daydream about things we hope will happen.

In verse 14, the psalmist has expressed his joy in the Word of God, so it's natural for him to meditate on it. It's his greatest treasure. Those who love their treasure constantly think about ways to increase it or enjoy it more. Or, they may be consumed with the fear of losing it.

Meditation digests the Word into nourishment for our spirits. It's like a cow grazing on green grass. She chews it and swallows it. Later, as she rests beneath a shady tree, the grass comes up and she chews it again and again. Each time she chews it she extracts a little more nourishment from it.

Nothing offers more nourishment for the soul than consistent meditation on what God has said and done. Those who meditate will have great success (Joshua 1:8), and will be like a fruitful tree growing by the river's edge (Ps.1:3), and will be profitable to others (I Tim. 4:15).

B. He Resolved to Reflect on God's Ways v. 15b

And contemplate Your ways. The word rendered "contemplate" is the same word translated "look unto" in verse 6. It means to focus and follow carefully with the eye. In verse 14, he speaks of rejoicing in the way of God's testimonies. He first meditates on the Lord's precepts, and then sharpens his focus on the ways which the precepts open to him.

When we focus our attention on His ways He shows us where the dangers are and helps us navigate around the traps the enemy sets for us. A woman on board a ship was afraid of rocks as the ship entered a narrow passage. She asked the captain if he knew where all the rocks were. "No," he replied," but I know where the deep water is." The ways revealed in God's Word will lead us away from the rocks and into the safety of deep waters.

> Thy Word I promise to ponder,
> For Thy precepts are always right.
> From Thy ways I will not wander,
> For to obey is my delight.

C. He Resolved to Rejoice in God's Word v.16a

I will delight myself in Your statutes. To delight is not the same as to rejoice. Rejoice is a festive word. Delight denotes a settled and continuing pleasure. The Word of God brings both. Notice he says, "I will delight myself." We can find delightful pleasure in God's Word when we are alone with it. When there is no sermon or song, no fellowship with others, we can still delight in God's Word. Some of my greatest joys have come when alone in my study and discovered some new insight into God's Word. Sometimes I've had to lay my Bible down, walk around the room and give thanks and glory to God for the wonders of His Word.

The psalmist resolves first to meditate, next to contemplate, and then to delight in the Word. When we meditate and contemplate, delight is sure to follow.

D. He Resolved to Remember God's Word v.16b

I will not forget Your Word. Memory is a sacred gift of God. To lose it is to suffer great loss. The word "forget" used here means to have memory softened or dimmed by time. We remember the things that delight us. The miser doesn't forget where he has buried his treasure. Our love for, and delight in, the Word of God, embeds it in our memories in a way that, even though we may forget other things, it will remain with us.

There's great danger in reading or hearing the Word of God and forgetting it."For if anyone is a hearer of the Word and not a doer, he is like a man observing his natural face in a mirror, for he observes himself, goes away and immediately forgets what kind of man he was" (James 1:23-24).

The four "I wills" of verses 15-16 follow the five "I haves" of verses 10-14. The psalmist makes resolutions for the future because of what grace has enabled him to do in the past. If grace has enabled us to accomplish things in the past, we can expect the Lord will give us grace to do even more in the future.

> I take pleasure in Thy sacred pages,
> And will never forget Thy Word,
> Though unchanged through the ages,
> Yet millions have still not heard.

STANZA 3: PSALM 119:17-24

THE SOLUTION TO LIFE'S STRESSES

I.   The Psalmist's Desires vs.17-18
   A. For Abundant Life v.17
   B. For Adequate Light v.18
II. The Psalmist's Distresses vs.19-20
   A. He is Distressed from Loneliness v.19
   B. He is Distressed from Longing v.20
III. The Psalmist's Detractors vs.21-23
   A. Who They Were v.21
   B. What They Did v.22-23
      1. They scorned him v.22
      2. They slandered him v.23
IV. The Psalmist's Discoveries v.24
   A. He Discovered Delight v.24a
   B. He Discovered Direction v.24b

Like all of us, the psalmist suffered from the stresses of life. Some of his stresses came from the intense passions and desires within him. Others grew out of his circumstances. In this stanza he describes how he finds solace in God's Word in all his experiences as a servant of God and a stranger on the earth.

I. THE PSALMIST'S DESIRES VS.17-18

A. For Abundant Life v.17

Deal bountifully with Your servant that I might live and keep Your word. The word translated 'deal bountifully" means to be generous or show favor in a manner that goes beyond merit. It suggests an act of God's grace. He wants God to deal with him based on God's goodness, not his own.

The psalmist refers to himself as a servant, and so puts himself in a position to receive God's grace. It suggests his readiness to submit, receive and learn.

He prays, not only for the preservation of his physical life, but for abundant life so he can more fully keep God's Word. Life comes before works. We are God's workmanship created unto good works. We have no power to obey His Word apart from the life He gives us. The psalmist's passion was to keep God's Word. He wanted his life extended so he could obey the Word.

Deal bountifully with me I plead.
Extend my life another day,
And so fulfill my greatest need
To hear Thy Word and obey.

B. For Adequate Light v.18

Open my eyes that I may see wondrous things from Your law. The Hebrew word *gaiah* translated "open" means to uncover or unveil, to take away that which prevents clear vision. We don't need plainer Scripture, but clearer eyes. Many study the Bible for years, may even teach it, without the veil ever being removed from their eyes. A blind man doesn't need a brighter sun. He needs sight to see the brightness of the one we have.

The psalmist's request suggests that only God can open our eyes to spiritual truth. The veil isn't on the Scriptures; it's on our hearts, and it can only be removed by the Holy Spirit. Without the Spirit's illumination the beauties of the Word remain shrouded in darkness. Paul said, "But even if our gospel is veiled, it is veiled to those who are perishing whose minds the god of this world has blinded" (I Cor. 4:3-4). In another place he said, "No one knows the things of God except the Spirit of God...We have received, not the spirit of the world, but the Spirit who is from God, that we might know the things that have been freely given us by God" (I Cor. 2:11-12). Later, he prayed for the saints at Ephesus that the eyes of their understanding might be opened that they might know the hope of God's calling (Eph. 1:18).

Wondrous things are extraordinary things, amazing things that are hidden from common view. The Scriptures are full of vast treasures that no one has yet seen, and mysteries that have never been explained.

These wonders are already in God's Word. They don't come to us through dreams and visions, or through prophecies privately given to those who claim some new visitation from God. We don't need more revelation. Instead we need our eyes opened to the revelation God has already given.

The psalmist's prayer doesn't exclude the need for diligent study. The prospector who is satisfied with panning a few gold nuggets from the stream will never discover the rich vein of yellow ore hidden deep in the mountainside. If we are satisfied with a few nuggets of truth picked up from sermons and Sunday school lessons, we'll never see the wondrous things from God's Word.

Someone has said a casual study of the Bible is like looking at an iceberg. You only see a small part of its truth. There's much more beneath the surface. G. Morgan Campbell, the great Bible teacher of the early 20th Century, said, "The Bible yields its treasures to honest toil more readily than does any other serious literature. But the Bible never yields to indolence."

Paul told Timothy, "Be diligent to present yourself approved to God, rightly dividing the word of truth" (II Tim. 2:15).

May the prayer of the psalmist for God to open his eyes to see the wondrous things in God's Word, be our prayer every time we open our Bibles!

O Lord, that I might see
Things that before have been sealed,
Things now unknown to me,
In Thy Word are revealed.

II. THE PSALMIST'S DISTRESSES
VS.19-20

A. He is Distressed from Loneliness v.19

I am a stranger in the earth; do not hide Your commandments from me. This is a plea for enlightenment from the Word. His first plea in verse 17 was based on his being a servant. This one is based on his being a stranger in a foreign place. In verse 18, his plea was "Open my eyes." In this verse, it's "Don't hide your commandments from me."

He's a stranger on earth. His citizenship is in heaven. Hebrews 11, tells us that the ancient patriarchs were strangers on earth who "all died in faith, not having received the promises, but having seen them afar off, were assured of them, embraced them, and confessed that they were strangers and pilgrims on earth"(Heb. 11:15).

We too, are strangers on earth. Our king is Jesus, who told Pilate, "My kingdom is not of this world" (John 18:36). He told His apostles they were to be in the world, but not of it. Being a stranger in a foreign land can be a very lonely experience if you don't know anyone, and can't speak the language. It can be especially lonely if it's a prolonged exile like the Israelites experienced in Babylon. They even hung their harps on the willows and cried, "How can we sing the Lord's song in a strange land" (Ps. 137:4)?

I remember how alone I felt when I got off the plane in Kiev, Ukraine just after the break-up of the Soviet Union. I knew only about 50 words of Russian. I couldn't read the signs, and no one was speaking English. Though surrounded by hundreds of people, I felt completely alone until I found my host and interpreter.

A stranger in a foreign country has no possessions there and no rights under law. The food is different and the customs are strange. It can be a very stressful experience. God's Word is like a letter from home to cheer us in a strange land.

When we're strangers in a foreign country we need a guide book and a map. The psalmist pleaded for God's commandments to guide and comfort him during his pilgrimage on earth. In the Word he found relief from the stress of being isolated in a strange land.

Although we are born into this world, we're strangers here. Its ways are contrary to the ways of our heavenly home. Its values are upside down. Our very existence incurs its disapproval, even its hatred. Like the psalmist, we need God's Word to guide us and comfort us in this strange land.

> Lord, I'm but a stranger here.
> Never depart from my side.
> And I will live without fear,
> With Thy Word as my guide.

B. He is Distressed from Longing v.20

My soul breaks with longing for Your judgments at all times. The Hebrew word *garas*, translated "breaks" means to break by rubbing, scraping or grating. His soul is not broken by a single blow; it's worn away little by little by his constant longing for the judgments of God. Like Job, he treasured the words of God's mouth more than his necessary food (Job 23:12). This breaking of the soul describes the passionate longing of a heart searching for God.

True holiness is found in a passion for God. We don't know who wrote this psalm, but this verse and others, reflect David's passion for God found in other psalms attributed to him. One is Psalm 42:1, "As the deer pants for the water brook, so pants my soul for You, O God." Another is, "O God, You are my God: early will I seek You. My soul thirsts for You. My flesh longs for You in a dry and thirsty land where there is no water" (Ps.88:1).

We'll never really discover the rich treasures of God's Word until our hearts break to know them. "He satisfies the longing soul and fills the hungry with goodness" (Ps.107:9). Jesus said, "Blessed are they that hunger and thirst after righteousness, for they shall be filled" (Matt. 5:6).

When we're born again our new natures gravitate toward the Word of God like a needle toward a magnet. When I was in college a Japanese seminary president spoke in one of our chapel services. He told how that someone gave him a Bible one day, and explained how Jesus had died for him. He said a great weight lifted from him so that he felt like he was floating. He said his heart was so powerfully drawn to it that he started reading the Bible in Genesis, and read all the way through it without eating or sleeping.

The psalmist was passionate about God's judgments. He longed for them constantly. Desire for the Word that comes and goes like the wind can scarcely be called a passion. They are temporary emotions born in times of excitement and die when the heat that aroused them cools.

> Lord, for Thy judgments I long.
> They are all my soul requires.
> They tell me what's right and wrong,
> And give me my heart's desires.

III. THE PSALMIST'S DETRACTORS
VS.21-23

A. Who They Were v.21

You rebuke the proud – the cursed, who stray from Your commandments. The proud have an inflated sense of their own importance. Some translations have used words such as haughty, insolent and over-bearing to describe them.

Pride is the root of all sin. It was the sin of Lucifer, who exalted himself above God (Isa. 14:12-5). Pride, not sexual perversion, was the chief sin of Sodom. "Look, this was the iniquity of your sister, Sodom. She and her daughter had pride, fullness of food and abundance of idleness; and they were haughty and committed abominations before Me" (Ezek. 16:49-50). Pride opened the doors of Sodom to all her other sins.

The proud, the arrogant and the haughty always stand in opposition to those who obey God's Word. There can be no agreement between the humble and the proud. There are irreconcilable differences between the God-centered, and the self-centered. The psalmist recognized this, and we see it clearly today. Those who call Christ Lord are a threat to those who believe they are the center of the universe. Today, the arrogant and the haughty would like to eliminate the name of God from all public places.

The proud are cursed without knowing it. They walk in slippery places and are marked for destruction. "Pride goes before destruction and a haughty spirit before a fall" (Prov. 16:18). And, "Before destruction the heart of a man is haughty, and before honor is humility" (Prov. 18:12). The seeds of destruction are contained in haughtiness. The proud are cursed by their own arrogance. It was true of Pharoah. It was true of Haman. It was true of Herod, and it's true today. We see it in political arrogance, in the pride of riches, in intellectual pride, the pride of sinful lifestyles and even religious pride. Regardless of the form, it's all under the curse of God, and will be destroyed.

But the psalmist was content to let God deal with the proud. "You rebuke the proud," was his prayer. They were cursed by God and God would deal with them in His own way and His own time just as He did with Sodom, Pharoah, Haman and Herod. We can rest in the promise that "God resists the proud, but gives grace to the humble" (I Peter 5:5).

The proud do not recognize God's commandments. To obey God would require them to give up their pride and humble themselves, something they will not do. They make up their own rules for living, which lead to their destruction.

Lord, against me they stand
With hearts haughty and proud.
Rebuke them now with Thy hand
Till every knee is bowed.

B. What They Did vs.22-23
   1. They scorned him v.22

*Remove from me reproach and contempt, for I
have kept Your testimonies.* The proud had heaped
reproach and contempt upon the psalmist. They were
not content just to disobey God's commandments
themselves they reproached those who did obey
them. The word "reproach" means to shame, scorn,
taunt, stigmatize and to hurl malicious words and
accusations at an enemy. "Contempt" means to disre-
spect, to insult or make a laughing stock of someone.
Jesus often suffered from the taunts of His enemies.
When he said the daughter of Jairus wasn't dead, but
sleeping, they ridiculed Him (Matt. 9:24). Even as
He died on the cross His enemies mocked Him.

All of us like to have others speak well of us,
so when we're the objects of ridicule, it's painful.
The psalmist asked the Lord to remove the reproach
and contempt of his enemies. The word translated
"remove" means to roll or drive something away. In
Joshua 3:9 God told Joshua, "This day I have rolled
away the reproach of Egypt from you." By bringing
the people into the land He had promised them, God
had removed the reproach the Egyptians had heaped
upon them.

When we're the objects of ridicule our natural
tendency is to strike back. We want to get even, or

vindicate ourselves by arguing or offering some defense. If we do, we'll only make the situation worse. The best way to deal with ridicule is to let the Lord deal with it in His own way. If He doesn't remove it He will give us the grace to bear it. We read in Hebrews 12:3 that Jesus, "who for the joy that was set before Him, endured the shame, and has sat down at the right hand of God." He endured the shame of the cross because He considered it as nothing compared to the joy set before Him. If we suffer the sting of ridicule and contempt, it's nothing compared to the eternal joy we have in heaven.

A clear conscience toward God softens the sting of scorn. The psalmist viewed his obedience to God's testimonies as grounds for asking the Lord to remove the reproach and contempt he was enduring. If we deserve the reproach we receive, we will have little confidence that God will remove it. However, reproach will not long remain on those who obey His commandments.

> They heaped upon me their scorn,
> And my heart felt its sharp sting
> Like the piercing of a thorn.
> Still to Thy Word I will cling.

2. They slandered him v.23

Princes also sit and speak against me, but Your servant meditates on Your statutes. Princes represent those in high places. – places of power and authority. The proud scorned him and the powerful slandered him. Those who should be the dispensers of justice conjured up evil accusations against him. He's not slandered and scorned in taverns and streets, but in the palaces of princes and kings. When the poor are slandered by the powerful the Lord is their only defense.

The psalmist was unmoved by what the powerful in high places said about him. Nothing distracted him from prayer and God's Word. He was not intimidated by their falsehoods.

The answer to the slanderous attacks of others isn't retaliation; it's meditation. We can't fight the devil and his henchmen with their own weapons. If we do, we'll lose. The psalmist knew that meditation on the Word of God would protect him from the plots of the powerful. Isaiah said, "No weapon formed against you shall prosper, and every tongue which rises against you in judgment, you shall condemn. This is the heritage of the servants of the Lord" (Isa. 54:17).

When the princes of Babylon plotted against Daniel, he was unmoved by their evil designs. He continued to pray at the same time and in the same place as he was accustomed to do, even though it meant being thrown into the lion's den. But their plot didn't succeed. Daniel was delivered and the plotters themselves were thrown to the lions (Dan. 6).

My name is held in contempt
By those seated in high places.
Yet they fail in every attempt
To find any truth in their cases.

IV. THE PSALMIST'S DISCOVERIES
V.24

A. He Discovered Delight v.24a

Your testimonies are my delight. The slanderers in high places couldn't take away the psalmist's delight in the Word of God. The more he meditated on it the more he delighted in it. He discovered the peace and joy that comes from clinging to God's Word even in times of great trouble. As mentioned in the comments on verse 16, delight signifies a settled and continuing pleasure in God's Word. The psalmist found that delight. May we also discover it!

B. He Discovered Direction v.24b

and my counselors. The Bible tells us to seek counsel from others, and we should. However, the best counsel is in the Word of God. But it's only when we meditate on it and find delight in it that we'll find counsel in it. Where could we find better counsel than from Moses, David, Solomon, Jesus and Paul?

To receive God's counsel and direction for life we must surrender our lives to Him. "In all your ways acknowledge Him and He will direct your paths" (Prov.3:6). Later in Psalm 119, the psalmist says, "Your Word is a lamp unto my feet and a light to my path" (v.107). We all need His direction because our own judgment is flawed. "There is a way that seems right to a man, but its end is the way of death" (Prov.14:12).

Thy Word is my delight;
From it I seek direction.
Its counsel is always right,
So I submit to its correction.

STANZA 4: PSALM 119:25-32

DEALING WITH DEPRESSION

I.   What He Prays When Depressed vs.25-28
He Prays for God:
   A. To Revive His Soul v.25
   B. To Repeat the Teaching of the Word v.26
       1. The report v.26a
       2. The response v.26b
       3. The request v.26c
   C. To Reveal to Him the Way v.27
       1. By illumination v.27a
       2. By meditation v.27b
   D. To Restore His Strength v.28
II. What He Pursues When Depressed vs.29-31
   A. He Pursues God's Truth vs.29-30
       1. He rejects lying v.29
       2. He receives the truth v.30
   B. He Pursues God's Testimonies v.31
III. What He Promises When Depressed v.32

A. A Promise Announced v.32a

B. A Provision Anticipated v.32b

The psalmist has gone from being distressed in the last stanza to being depressed to the point of despair in this one. He's beaten down and has come to the end of his own strength. Because of his prayer that he might live in verses 17 and 25, some commentators have suggested that he might have been sick. Perhaps the reproach and slander by his enemies had worn him down. Maybe it was the longing and the loneliness. We just don't know. Sometimes there are no clear reasons for depression.

While he doesn't tell us the cause of his depression, he does tell us the cure. In his desperate condition he resorts to prayer and the Word of God. That's what this stanza is all about.

I. WHAT HE PRAYS WHEN DEPRESSED
VS. 25-28

He prays for God:

A. To Revive His Soul v.25

My soul clings to the dust; Revive me according to Your word. The word translated "cling" means to be glued or stuck fast. In Old Testament times those in mourning sat in dust and ashes and put dust on their heads, or lay prostrate in the dust. In Psalm 44:25 David wrote, "Our soul is bowed down to the dust. Our body clings to the ground." The psalmist identified with Job who said, "My flesh is caked with worms and dust" (Job 7:8).

The psalmist prays that he might be revived 11 times in Psalm 119. The word means to restore life, to recover or to refresh. The King James Version translates it "quicken." The writer has had the breath knocked out of him by the circumstances of life. Lying in the dust, he calls on God to revive him. Only God, who gave life in the beginning, can restore it.

When we have been knocked down, we need for God to revive and refresh us. In Psalm 71:20, David cried, "You who have shown me great and severe troubles, shall revive me again and bring me up from the depths of the earth." And in Psalm 143:11 he said, "Revive me O God for Your name's sake! For your righteousness sake, bring my soul out of trouble." In Psalm 23:3, he said the Lord "restores my soul."

The psalmist asks the Lord to revive him according to His Word. The Word has power to revive. Hebrews 4:12 says, "For the word of God is living and powerful, and sharper than any two-edged sword…" And in verse 50 of this psalm we read, "Your word has given me life." There is life-giving power in the Word of God.

The Spirit also gives life. Jesus said, "It is the Spirit who gives life. The words that I speak to you are spirit and they are life" (John 6:63). The Spirit gives life but the Word is the vehicle of the Spirit to bring it. We are revived by the interaction of the Spirit and the Word in our hearts. It's possible to read and study the Word and not experience its reviving power because the Spirit is not allowed to do His work in us. If the Word and the Spirit are separated there is no life.

> Lord, from the dust I cry;
> All my strength is gone.
> I look with longing eye
> To Thee and Thee alone.

B. To Repeat the Teaching of the Word v.26
  1. The report v.26a
I have declared my ways. The word "declare" infers a numbering or a listing. The psalmist is giving God a complete report. His depression prompted a detailed self-examination, and he reported to God everything he discovered. His report, no doubt, included a confession of his sins. Depression usually leads us to search for reasons. In the process of searching we often come face to face with our sins. Before we can ask God to teach us His Word, we must ask Him to cleanse us of our sins.

In addition to his sins the psalmist reported his cares, his disappointments, his problems, his sorrows, his hopes, his feelings and his dreams. He held nothing back. He laid everything out before God. There's nothing we can't bring to the Lord in prayer. Paul said, "Be anxious for nothing, but in EVERYTHING by prayer and supplication, with thanksgiving, let your requests be made known to God" (Phil. 4:6).

We are invited to come boldly before the throne of grace because in Christ we have a High Priest who can sympathize with our weaknesses because

He experienced the same temptations that we experience, yet without sin (Heb. 4:15-16).

2. The response v.26b

And You answered me. God responded to his report with an answer. We don't know what the answer was. Perhaps it was assurance of forgiveness and acceptance before God, and confidence that the Lord would lift him up out of the dust. When we approach God in faith, and lay our lives open to Him, we can be sure He will hear us. "And if we know He hears us, whatever we ask, we know that we have the petitions that we have asked Him" (I John 5:15).

3. The request v.26c

Teach me Your statutes. The psalmist made this same request in verse 12, and he will make it four more times before the psalm is finished. Every time he repeats the request the circumstances surrounding it are a little different. In verse 12, he makes the request after looking at God. Here, he makes the request after looking at himself. There's never a time when we feel a greater need for God to teach us than after a time of honest self-examination.

> I told Him all of my grief,
> And laid before Him my fears.
> He heard me and sent relief,
> Whispering His Word in my ears.

C. To Reveal to Him the Way v.27
  1. Through illumination v.27a

Make me to understand the way of Your precepts.
He asks the Lord to make him understand because he
is incapable of understanding them on his own. We
can analyze the grammar, define the words and grasp
what it says, but that doesn't mean we understand
the way of His precepts. Many unbelieving teachers
teach the letter of the Word without any illumination
of the Spirit. Paul said, "But the natural man does
not receive the things of the Spirit of God, nor can he
know them because they are spiritually discerned"
(I. Cor. 2:14).

  2. Through meditation v.27b

So shall I meditate on Your wonderful works. In
verse 15, the psalmist promised to meditate on God's
precepts. Now he vows to meditate on God's works.
One of the definitions for meditate is to mutter or
speak to oneself. Some translators translate it "speak."
In that case, he would be saying, "I shall speak of
Your wonderful works." That would be appropriate
here. However, most translations say "meditate" and
I'll stick with that.

His meditation on God's works seems to depend
on his ability to understand the way of the Lord's
precepts. Those who have no insight into God's Word
usually don't recognize His works. Those who don't
understand what He has said won't see what He has
done. The evolutionist who denies what God's Word
says about creation doesn't see His handiwork in
the world. Those who have no understanding of the

Bible won't recognize God's hand working among
His people.

Lord, it's Thy way that I choose.
Help me to understand
That my heart may daily muse
On the works of Thy hand.

D. To Restore His Strength v.28

*My soul melts from heaviness; strengthen me
according to Your word.* The psalmist records the
inner life of his soul. In verse 20 he says, "My soul
breaks." In verse 25 he says, "My soul clings to the
dust," Here he says, "My soul melts." The Hebrew
word translated "melts" means to drip, to drop or
distill. It's usually a poetic expression for weeping.
It suggests a steady flow of tears that eventually
dissolves or wears down the soul.

After a great victory at Jericho, the armies of
Israel were soundly defeated by the little town of Ai
a few days later. The Bible says, "The hearts of the
people melted and became like water" (Josh. 7:5).
Psalm 107:26, says, "They go down into the depths;
their soul melts because of trouble."

The psalmist was having a soul meltdown because
of his depression. His tears were distilled sorrow.
The longer trouble lingers the heavier the burden
becomes. Any continuing sorrow or trouble can
wear us down. It can be family problems, financial
problems, disappointments, losses or even longings
and desires for good things. The psalmist's soul was
broken by longing for God's judgments in verse 20.

Paul had great sorrow and continual grief in his heart for the salvation of his fellow Jews (Rom. 9:3).

The word "strengthen" literally means to lift up. Sometimes God lifts the burden from us. At other times He strengthens us by an infusion of His grace that enables us to bear the burden without being crushed by it.

The psalmist asks for strength according to God's Word. Perhaps he remembered God's promise in Deuteronomy 33:25, "As your days are so shall your strength be." God's Word is filled with promises of strength. "Wait upon the Lord; be of good courage, and He will strengthen your heart. Wait I say upon the Lord" (Psalm 27:14). Isaiah said, He gives power to the weak, and to those who have no might He increases strength... Those who wait upon the Lord shall renew their strength. They shall mount up with wings like eagles. They shall run and not be weary. They shall walk and not faint" (Isa. 40:29,31).

> My sorrow is without end;
> My grief knows no bounds.
> I pray Thy strength to send,
> And restore the joyful sounds.

II. WHAT HE PURSUES WHEN DEPRESSED VS. 29-31

A. He Pursues God's Truth Vs.29-30
   1. He rejects lying v.29
   Remove from me the way of lying and grant me Thy law graciously. He doesn't pray that he will be

removed from the way of lying, but that the way of lying will be removed from him. It's not a request to get him out of the trap, but to remove the trap from him. He wanted the way of lying removed just as we would want a poisonous snake or a raging lion removed from our houses.

The way of lying is the way of the world. All the world's promises of happiness, fulfillment and pleasure are lies. Lying is the accepted practice of the world. Politicians lie, the media lie, business men lie, advertisers lie, lawyers lie, brokers lie, witnesses lie, the police lie, and even the government lies.

We even lie to ourselves, which is perhaps the worst lie of all. We deceive ourselves and believe our own lies. We even try to lie to God. Lying is a sin we all fall into, so this is a prayer we all must pray.

Unfortunately, many view lying as did the young boy who was asked in Sunday school to give a definition of lying. "A lie is an abomination unto the Lord and a very present help in time of trouble," he answered.

Jesus said the devil is a liar and the father of lies (John 8:44). However, man's heart is the place where lies are stored and his mouth their main distribution point.

The psalmist wanted to replace the way of lying with God's law. The law is a reservoir of truth, so it's contrary to the way of lying. He regarded the law as a gracious gift of God. He thought of it as a way of deliverance from the power of falsehood. If the law filled his heart with truth, lies would not enter.

Let me no longer deceive;
Remove this deadly flaw,
And grant that I might cleave
To Thy true and gracious law

2. He receives the truth v.30

I have chosen the way of truth, Your judgments I have laid before me. To reject something is to choose its opposite. So to reject lying is to choose the truth. To choose light is to reject darkness. To reject evil is to choose the good. Lying is natural, but truth is something we must choose.

It's not enough to accept the doctrinal truths of the Bible. God demands inward truth and honesty. David, after confessing his sin with Bathsheba, said, "Behold, You desire truth in the inward parts" (Ps.51:5). Inward truth means an end to self deception.

When we choose the way of truth we'll no longer just follow our feelings and impulses, or the mores of our culture. God's Word will be our guide. If we decide to take a trip we usually lay out a map and plan our route. The psalmist chose to follow the way of truth and laid out the judgments of God as his guide for living. The word "judgments" suggests a standard for distinguishing between good and evil. If we choose the way of truth we must obey the Word of God because God's words are truth just as God is truth.

Thy truth is what I desire.
I have made it my choice.
To Thy judgments I aspire,
In them I greatly rejoice.

B. He Pursues God's Testimonies v.31

I cling to Your testimonies; O Lord, do not put me to shame! The word "cling" is the same one used in v.25. Now, instead of clinging to the dust, the psalmist is clinging to the Word of God. He has made a deliberate choice to walk in the way of truth, and he's sticking with the instruction manual.

No matter what his thoughts are, or how he feels, he clings to the one thing that will never change. It's a lesson we all should learn. No matter what the latest theory may be, what the media may tell us, or what the polls say, we should cling to what the Word of God says. It's never wrong, and it will never change.

In his depressed condition the fear of shame once again arises within him. If he clings to the Lord's testimonies he will never be put to shame. That could happen only if God's promises failed. We never need to be ashamed when we walk in the way of truth and hold fast to His Word.

In times of sorrow, suffering and stress, we're prone to grow impatient and act foolishly. Maybe that's what the psalmist feared. We can avoid attitudes and actions that lead to shame by clinging to God's Word. We would do well to follow the example of Isaiah. "For the Lord will help me. Therefore, I will not be disgraced. Therefore, I have set my face like a flint, and I know that I will not be ashamed" (Isa.50:7).

Paul had the same assurance when he said, "For this reason I also suffer these things: nevertheless, I am not ashamed, for I know whom I have believed and am persuaded that He is able to keep what I have committed to Him until that day" (II Tim. 1:12).

In his depression the psalmist pursued truth and clung to the Word of God. So should we!

Though I in sorrow grieve,
I will never be ashamed,
For to Thy Word I cleave,
To every promise named.

III. WHAT HE PROMISES WHEN DEPRESSED V.32

A. A Promise Announced v.32a
I will run the course of Your commandments. Running suggests progress, freedom and eagerness. He's saying he's excited about keeping God's commandments. He will do it with all his energy. He begins this stanza clinging to the dust, but now he's ready to run in the way of truth. His faith looks beyond the dust and tears to running with eagerness and joy. His strength is gone, but by faith he promises to run.

B. A Provision Anticipated v.32b
For You shall enlarge my heart. To enlarge the heart is to free it from hindrances. In this case, it

means to remove the depression. He couldn't run until the burden was lifted. His enlarged heart meant greater energy and an increased desire to walk in the way of truth. He's eager to obey as the Lord gives him strength. If you're burned out and burdened down; if your strength is gone and you're clinging to the dust, choose the way of truth. He will enlarge your heart and restore you so that you may run with new freedom and joy.

Out of the dust I will rise
To run with eager heart,
That I might win the prize,
And joy will not depart.

THE PRAYER OF A NEEDY SAINT

I. He Asked God to Repeat the Instructions vs. 33-34

   He promised to:

   A. Obey Continually v.33
   B. Obey Completely v.34

II. He Asked God to Reinforce His Intentions vs. 35-36

   A. Regarding His Walk v.35
   B. Regarding His Wants v.36

III. He Asked God to Resolve His Issues vs. 37-39

   A. By Redirecting His Eyes v.37
   B. By Reestablishing the Word in Him v.38
   C. By Removing His Fears v.39
      Conclusion: v. 40

This stanza reflects the psalmist's desire to obey the Lord's commandments and live a holy life. The entire stanza is a prayer with a variety of requests, all to help him obey. There is sense of urgency in his requests. Perhaps it reflects the eagerness of the enlarged heart he received as he emerged from his depression in the previous stanza.

I. HE ASKED GOD TO REPEAT THE INSTRUCTIONS VS.33-34

In these verses he is promising God that if He will repeat the instructions, he'll get it right this time. He promises:

A. To Obey Continually v.33
Teach me O Lord, the way of Your statutes, and I will keep them to the end. He repeats his prayer for God to teach him. It's a prayer that we all need to repeat every day because we need repetition to learn. The same lessons sometimes need to be repeated over and over. Then, there's always new truth to learn, even from the same Scripture. We need to go over them again and again and ask the Lord to teach us. The key to learning new truth is to obey the truth we already know. In verses 33 and 34, the psalmist again asks the Lord to teach him, and promises to obey what he learns.

The Hebrew word translated "teach" means to point out with the hand, to indicate or to show. We don't have to be taught to sin. We learn it without any teaching. But we have to be taught to do right.

The more we're taught the Word the more we feel the need to be taught. So teaching is an ongoing need in our lives.

The psalmist isn't just asking the Lord to teach him what the statutes are. He wants to learn the WAY of the statutes. God's statutes mark the road to a holy life.

There's a way to do everything. There's a way to play baseball. There's a way to drive a car. In most things we do certain steps must be followed. If we don't follow them we will fail. So it is with the Christian life. God's Word is the instruction manual for holy living. But we must do more than read it, analyze it and memorize it. We must follow its directions. In Psalm 32:8 we read, "I will instruct you and teach you in the way you should go; do not be like the horse or like the mule, which have no understanding, which must be harnessed with bit and bridle."

Governments pass statutes designed to govern our behavior. Sometimes these statutes may seem irksome or even foolish. Not so with God's statutes. "The statutes of the Lord are right, rejoicing the heart. The commandments of the Lord are pure, enlightening the eyes" (Ps.19:6).

A lifelong commitment to obey the Lord's statutes accompanies the psalmist's request for teaching. His commitment was made before the teaching was done. He pledged unconditional and continual obedience to the statutes regardless of how difficult it might me. We don't receive the truth and then decide whether or not to obey it. If we don't commit to obeying it we won't receive it. We must obey the truth we know before we receive more. This means continued teaching and continued obedience to the end of our lives.

> Lord, shine Thy light on me.
> Help me keep Thy ways,
> And Thy faithful servant be
> Til the end of my days.

B. To Obey Completely v.34

Give me understanding and I shall keep Your law; Indeed, I shall observe it with my whole heart. Understanding is a step above knowledge. It involves the ability to discern, especially between good and evil. Paul told the Colossians, "We...do not cease to pray for you, and ask that you might be filled with the knowledge of His will and all wisdom and understanding" (Co. 1:9). Job said, "The fear of the Lord, that is wisdom, and to depart from evil is understanding" (Job 28:28).

Any writer or teacher can give us information, but understanding is from God. "We know that the Son of God has come and has given us an understanding" (I John 5:20). God doesn't give us understanding in order that we might display our wisdom, but that we might obey Him.

The psalmist promised to observe the law with all his heart. The word translated "observe" means to give careful attention to something. Obedience was not a casual effort to him. As he has done before, he promised to obey wholeheartedly. His heart is focused on obedience to God's Word.

Lord, teach me to understand
The wisdom of Thy way,
And to observe every command,
And with my whole heart obey.

II. HE ASKED GOD TO REINFORCE HIS INTENTIONS VS.35-36

A. Regarding His Walk v.35

Make me to walk in the path of Your command-ments, for I delight in it. First the psalmist asked for light that he might understand. Now he is asking for strength to walk in the light. It's not a lack of will-ingness but a lack of ability that hinders him. We are powerless to obey what we have been taught. Only by God's grace can we walk in the path of His commandments

His plea is for God to make him do what he can't do for himself. To walk in the path of God's command-ments needs more discipline than he possesses, so he pleads for God to reinforce his desires and his inten-tions. Like Paul, he is saying, "For to will is present in me, but how to perform what is good I do not find" (Rom.7:18).

It's our cry too, but God is our enabler. "For it is God who works in you to will and to do for His good pleasure"(Phil. 2:13). Just as surely as God can give us the will to obey, He can give us the power to obey.

The psalmist delighted in the way of God's commandments. We can only ask God to make us do what we want to do. He will only help us obey if we want to obey. Psalm 37:23 says, "The steps of a good man are ordered by the Lord, and He delights in his way." And Psalm 40:8 says, "I delight to do Your will O my God, and Your law is written in my heart." When we delight in His ways the Lord delights in us and gives us the power to walk in the path of His commandments.

> To walk in Thy path I vow.
> I delight in Thy Word every hour,
> But to keep it I know not how,
> Except by Thy grace and power.

B. Regarding His Wants v.36
Incline my heart to Your testimonies, and not to covetousness. To incline simply means to turn or turn about. Driving across the great plains of the American West, I've sometimes noticed that the trees all lean in the same direction because of the prevailing winds from the southwest. Even when the wind isn't blowing, the trees still lean because of the lifelong force of the wind against them. Virgil said, "As the twig is bent so the tree inclines." The lifelong force of sin inclines our hearts toward evil, and our actions follow our inclinations.

The psalmist is asking the Lord to change the inclinations of his heart. He wants his heart reprogrammed so that it will lean toward God's testimonies rather than toward covetousness. If you place a plant in a room near a window, it will soon lean toward the window because it is seeking the light.

He is asking the Lord to incline his heart toward the light.

It's not clear whether he mentioned the inclination toward covetousness because he felt that leaning, or because covetousness is the egg from which most sins hatch. "You shall not covet," is the 10th and last commandment (Ex. 20:17), but it's certainly not the least.

Covetousness is the natural inclination of the human heart. Paul had a problem with covetousness, and was convicted by it (Rom. 7:7). A covetous man wants what he can't have and desires what is not his. Only God can change it. Achan, Ahab, Balaam, Judas and thousands of others have seen their lives destroyed by it. But Christ changed the heart of Zacchaeus and inclined it away from covetousness to generosity (Luke 19).

Covetousness is totally incompatible with service to Christ and obedience to His Word. Jesus said, "You cannot serve God and mammon" (Luke 16:13). Paul summed up the tragedy of covetousness in I Timothy 16:13. "But those who desire to be rich fall into temptation and a snare, and into many foolish and harmful lusts which drown men in destruction and perdition. For the love of money is the root of all kind of evil, for which some have strayed from the faith in their greediness, and pierce themselves through with many sorrows."

The psalmist wanted to walk in God's path where no covetousness lurks, so he asks God to bend his heart away from covetousness and incline it toward God's testimonies.

Show me line upon line
The teachings of Thy law.
To it may my heart incline,
And all greed withdraw.

III. HE ASKED GOD TO RESOLVE HIS
ISSUES VS. 37-39

A. By Redirecting His Eyes v.37

Turn away my eyes from looking at worthless things, and revive me in Your way. If the psalmist was troubled by covetousness it was due to what his eyes had seen. His first issue to be resolved is an issue with his eyes. If the eyes don't see a thing, the heart is less likely to desire it. Our eyes are the devil's favorite gate to our souls.

It was through the eyes that sin first entered the world. "When Eve SAW that the tree was good for food she took it and ate" (Gen.3:6). Achan said, "When I SAW among the spoils a beautiful Babylonian garment, two hundred shekels of silver and a wedge of gold weighing fifty shekels, I coveted them and took them" (Josh. 7:21). David SAW Bathsheba bathing on the roof and sent for her (II Sam.11:2). One of the three things John warns believers about in I John 2:6 is the lust of the eyes.

The psalmist prays that his eyes will be turned away, not closed. We can't live with our eyes closed, and if they are open we will see evil. "Turn away" here means to look past without lingering. The King James Version has a better translation when it says, "Turn away my eyes from beholding vanity." The psalmist is praying that God will make his eyes pass quickly and not linger until looking turns into lust and lust into longing. He doesn't want his eyes to linger on worthless things or vanity. The Hebrew word translated "worthless things" means something that disappoints the hope it inspires – things without substance that arouse hope and expectation but deliver nothing of value.

We live in a world of vanity. The media is the main channel into our homes and into our eyes. Its message is, drink this kind of beer, buy this car, eat this food, exercise on this machine and you'll be as beautiful as the person you see on the screen. You'll live in a big house, have great friends and a happy life. We are aware that it's all vanity, but if we linger on it, it will poison us. Imagination and fantasy are stronger than the will.

In the story, "The Name of the Rose," a young priest brought a copy of Aristotle's "Poetics" into the monastery library. The abbot discovered the book and forbade the monks to read it. He hid it in an obscure place and put poison on its pages to guarantee that no one would read it. As the reader would touch his fingers to his tongue to moisten them in order to turn the pages, the poison would be transferred to his mouth. Decades later, two young monks discovered the book and slowly died a painful death.

Many Christians are destroying their spiritual lives little by little with the poison that enters their eyes through their TV sets and computers each day.

The psalmist wants to look beyond worthless things to a way of life that's real, to things of substance that deliver what they promise. The things that are real are often unseen by the eye. Faith allows us to see the unseen for it is "the substance of things hoped for, the evidence of things unseen" (Heb. 11:1).

Each of us should answer the question asked by the writer of Proverbs who asked, "Will you set your eyes upon that which is not" (Prov. 23:5)?

> O Lord, remove from my sight
> Things that are worthless and vain,
> That I might walk in the light,
> The wisdom of Thy ways to gain.

B. By Reestablishing the Word in Him v. 38

Establish Your word to Your servant who is devoted to fearing You. The psalmist's second issue revolves around his confidence in God's Word. Perhaps his confidence has been shaken by the grief and slander he has endured. His heart is desperately seeking God, but doubts may be arising regarding the promises of God. Such is the experience of many of God's choice servants. There are times when our experiences may shake our faith.

However, he may not be experiencing serious doubts about God's Word at all. He may just want confirmation of his faith. He has been undergoing tough times and is hurting. Maybe he just needed assurance from God as a child who is hurting needs assurance from its father. Whatever may have been the case, he took his doubts or need for affirmation to God.

The word "establish" means to lift up or make firm. It's the same word translated strengthen in verse 25. It suggests to make valid, to confirm or to ratify. Some translations say confirm. The confirmation he seeks may come from some outward sign, the fulfillment of something promised, or from an inward assurance. In Psalm 57:3 David voices a similar prayer when he says, "I will cry out to God, Most High, to God who performs (establishes) all things to me."

His request for God to confirm His Word to him seems to be based on his fear of God. He is not a casual follower or a backslider, but a devoted God fearing servant. Yet he needs affirmation of the truth of God's Word.

The whole argument is that those who serve the Lord and fear Him, may come boldly to Him with their hurts and even their doubts.

Make Thy Word sure in me.
Affirm with evidence clear
All I have heard from Thee,
For it's only Thee I fear.

C. By Removing His Fears v.39

Turn away my reproach which I dread for Your judgments are good. The psalmist's third issue concerns his fear of reproach. There two kinds of reproach. One is the mocking and scorn which believers may experience because of their faith. This is the kind of reproach the psalmist asked God to remove from him in verse 22.

The other kind is the reproach resulting from the inconsistent lives of believers. It's the kind that makes us stumbling blocks to unbelievers. Perhaps this is the reproach the psalmist dreaded most. It's what every Christian should dread. No believer wants to cause others to stumble by his or her behavior.

The word "turn away" is the same word used in verse 37, when he prayed, "Turn away my eyes." As explained in verse 37, the word means to look past or not linger. He is asking God to look past his reproach and help him get beyond it. This kind of reproach tends to linger in the minds of those who experience it. Only God can get us past it.

Since we don't know who the writer is we don't know what brought reproach on him. If David was the writer it could have been his adultery with Bathsheba and the murder of her husband which was a public disgrace and gave occasion to the enemies of the Lord to blaspheme (II Sam. 12:13).

This verse offers hope to those of us who have brought reproach upon ourselves and upon the Lord. That reproach need not remain on us forever. We can get past it. David did, as did Peter who denied the Lord. So have others. They did so by repentance followed by humble and obedient service. That doesn't mean there isn't a price to pay, or that no scars will remain. It just means that we can get past it and still be useful in Christ's service.

If the world would only attribute the evil we do to us we could more easily bear the reproach. But to our sorrow, our sin causes unbelievers to heap scorn on Christ. Our inconsistent lives give the world an occasion to say that God's Word is false and his followers are hypocrites.

Since God's judgments are good, if we obey them we need never fear bringing reproach upon ourselves and the cause of Christ. Peter summed it up in I Peter 4:14-16. "If you are reproached for the name of Christ blessed are you...but let none of you suffer as a murderer, a thief, an evildoer or as a busybody in other people's matters. Yet if anyone suffer as a Christian let him not be ashamed."

We should welcome reproach for doing good, but fear the reproach that comes from wrongdoing.

> Help me past the dread
> Of reproach I have brought
> By the words I have said
> And the deeds I have wrought.

Conclusion v.40

Behold, I long for Your precepts; revive me in Your righteousness. This verse is a summary and conclusion of his prayer. He has fought the battle of the eyes, been plagued with doubts and haunted by the fear of reproach. Still, he longs for God's precepts. He has a passion for the Word of God. He hasn't attained perfection, but he longs for it. Everybody wants to go to heaven, but few long to live by God's Word on the earth.

The psalmist wants the Lord to restore him to right living – living according to the precepts he longs for. If he lives according to these precepts he won't be inclined to covetousness, nor will his eyes linger on worthless things. He won't be paralyzed by doubts or live in dread of reproach.

"The fears of the wicked will come upon him, but the desire of the righteous will be granted" (Prov.10:24).

For Thy precepts I long.
I want to do what is right,
So turn my heart from wrong
And help me walk in the light.

STANZA 6: PSALM 119:41-48

FINDING HOPE IN GOD'S WORD

I. Experiencing the Provisions of God's Word vs.41-42
   A. It Provides Deliverance v.41
   B. It Provides Defense v. 42
II. Explaining the Prominence of God's Word vs.43-44
   A. Its Place v.43
   B. Its Persistence v.44a
   C. Its Permanence v.44b
III. Exercising the Power of God's Word vs.45-46
   A. He Walks Freely v.45
   B. He Talks Fearlessly v.46
IV. Enjoying the Pleasures of God's Word v.47-48
   A. He Declares His Joy v.47
   B. He Demonstrates His Joy v.48

1. Externally v.48a
2. Internally v.48b

The psalmist has been walking in darkness. He has been distressed, depressed and desperate, but he has not lost his grip on the Word. Now he prays for mercy, and hope begins to dawn. Mercy is the tree upon which hope grows. Every verse in this stanza unfolds the benefits of the mercies mentioned in verse 41.

The verses all begin with the Hebrew letter *waw*, which is equivalent to the English conjunction "and." So each verse is a link in a chain of mercies. The stanza is in the future tense. It's full of "I shalls" and "I wills," and pictures the benefits the psalmist hopes to receive from God through His Word.

I. EXPERIENCING THE PROVISIONS OF GOD'S WORD VS. 41-42

A. It Provides Deliverance v.41

Let Your mercies come also to me O Lord—Your salvation according to Your word. Spurgeon said, "He desired mercy as well as teaching because he was guilty as well as ignorant." He needed more than one, so he asked God to let "mercies" come to him. The channel of mercy seemed to be blocked, so he asked God to remove the blockage and allow His mercies to flow. The Bible says God is "plenteous" in mercy (Ps. 86:15), that He has "manifold" mercies (Neh. 9:19), and "multitudes of mercies" (Ps. 69:16). His compassions are "new every morning" (Lam. 3:23), and Paul said that He was "rich in mercy" (Eph. 3:4). There is an endless supply of God's mercies.

The psalmist connects God's mercies with his salvation. Keep in mind that the word "salvation" simply means rescue or deliverance, so it doesn't always mean salvation in the sense we use it today. Here it probably means deliverance from the darkness of his soul described in the previous three stanzas.

God's deliverances are always because of His mercy and come to us according to His Word. His mercies are never given in a manner that conflicts with His Word. They are in harmony with the plans God has for the world and for each of us individually as revealed in His Word. God will not act in a way that contradicts His laws or violates His will.

He gives mercy because He has promised mercy. When God promises to do something, He does it. Since He has given mercy to others we can expect Him to be merciful to us also. Perhaps the psalmist was thinking of the many mercies God had given to those he read about in the Word when he prayed, "Let Your mercies come ALSO to me." Since others have received God's mercies, he is encouraged to expect God to be merciful to him too.

God's mercies and deliverances are abundant, but He doesn't extend them to the proud and the unrepentant. He also chooses the manner of His deliverances, which may not be according to our expectations.

Lord, my soul needs refreshing.
Send Thy salvation to me.
Let fall the showers of blessing,
According to Thy Word let it be.

B. It Provides Defense v.42

So shall I have an answer for him who reproaches me, For I trust in Your word. The "so" that introduces this verse indicates that the answers for reproach grow out of what was said in the previous verse. That is, they come from God's grace and His Word. The phrase "For I trust in Your Word" in this verse reinforces that idea. "For" is to be understood in the sense of "because." So he has an answer because he trusts in God's Word.

Too often we try to answer the taunts hurled at us with reasoning and logic. We try to defend ourselves with arguments. It doesn't work! The enemies of God aren't enemies because it's reasonable, so they won't be changed by our arguments.

For example, those who believe the evolutionary view of creation don't believe it because it's reasonable. It's not! They do it because they don't want to admit the existence of God and be accountable to Him. It's a spiritual issue, not one of logic or even science. It grows out of their unbelief. You can't answer unbelief with arguments or fight the devil with carnal weapons. Proverbs 26:5 says, "Do not answer a fool according to his folly, lest you also be like him."

Paul said, "The weapons of our warfare are not carnal, but mighty in God for the pulling down of strongholds, casting down arguments and every high thing that exalts itself against the knowledge of God, bringing every thought into captivity to the obedience of Christ" (II Cor. 10:4-5).

The answers given in verse 41 which the psalmist (and we) can give to confound those who reproach us are: (1) his testimony of the mercies and deliverances he has experienced, and (2) the Word of God.

Paul was mocked and persecuted everywhere he went. His defense was always to reason with them from the Scriptures (not human reasoning) and to give a testimony of his salvation experience on the Damascus Road. Our enemies can't refute our testimonies. They may deny that God's Word is true and refuse to accept it, but even then the Spirit can use it to convict them.

John Phillips tells of a young boy who had been saved by reading John 3:16. In the bed that night doubts arose. Was it true? Was he really saved? Finally, he concluded that it was the devil tormenting him. He had been told that the devil loved darkness, and since the darkest place in his room was under his bed, perhaps the devil was lurking there. So he opened his Bible to John 3:16 and thrust the open Bible under the bed and said, "Here, read it for yourself."

God's Word is effective in defending us against reproach, but only if we trust in it. We don't need to defend the Word. It can defend itself, but if we doubt the Word, our defense is destroyed.

My answers always amaze
The scorners and unjust,
For Thy mercies light my ways,
And in Thy Word I trust

II. EXPLAINING THE PROMINENCE OF GOD'S WORD VS. 43-44

A. The Place of God's Word v.43

And take not the word of truth utterly out of my mouth, for I have hoped in Your ordinances. This is the only time the Word is called the word of truth in the Old Testament. The expression is used four times in the New Testament. The psalmist doesn't want it removed from his mouth. The best location for God's Word is in the mouth. This apparently means always present, always near. It's like our expression, "on the tip of the tongue." This is clear from Deuteronomy 30:12-14.

"For this commandment which I command you today is not too mysterious for you, nor is it far off. It is not in heaven that you should say, 'who will ascend to heaven and bring it down to us that we might hear it?' Nor is it beyond the sea that you should say, 'Who will go over the sea for us and bring it to us?' But the Word is very near you in your mouth and in your heart that you may do it."

God told Joshua, "This book of the law shall not depart from your mouth, but you shall meditate on it day and night that you may observe to do all that is written in it." (Josh. 1:8). Here it is connected with meditation which, among other things, means muttering or speaking to oneself.

When the Word is in our mouths it is constantly in our minds and hearts and we are ready to speak it for our defense or the instruction of others. We should always be able to give answers appropriate for any occasion. Jesus frequently silenced the Pharisees by quoting Scripture that was right for the occasion.

We can't give appropriate answers from the Word if we have to look them up in a concordance. The only concordance the psalmist had was the one in his heart. Peter said, "Always be ready to give a defense to anyone who asks you the reason for the hope that is in you with meekness and fear" (I Peter 3:15).

In verse 42, the psalmist trusts the Word. Now he hopes in it. If the Word is completely taken away he will have no answer for those who reproach him and all hope will be gone. He is beginning to climb out of the darkness. He has been clinging to the Word, and it's beginning to bring him hope for the future. If it's taken away he'll have no future.

Don't let Thy Word depart
My mouth or my lips.
Let it never leave my heart,
My hope to eclipse.

B. The Persistence of God's Word v.44a

So shall I keep Your law continually. To have God's Word in his mouth meant he was ready to obey it. God told Joshua not to let it depart from his mouth but to observe to do all that was written in it. We are to obey it without interruption in all places, at all times, under all circumstances. There are no holidays or vacations from obedience to God's Word.

C. The Permanence of God's Word v.44b

For ever and ever. The Hebrew language is limited in its ability to communicate abstract concepts like time. The best translation of this phrase is probably "for time and eternity." Jesus said, "Heaven and earth shall pass away but My words shall never pass away" (Matt. 24:35). As long as His Word exists we are to continue to obey it. So keeping His Word will never end.

I will obey to the end of days
All that Thy Word commands,
And give to Thee my praise,
When earth no longer stands.

III. EXERCISING THE POWER OF GOD'S WORD VS.45-46

A. He Will Walk Freely v.45

I will walk at liberty, for I seek Your precepts. Luther translates the first part of this verse, "I will walk freely." The word "liberty" comes from a Hebrew word meaning a wide place. It conveys the idea of without limits or restraints. There are many narrow and deep canyons in Israel. Some are hundreds of feet deep and only a few feet wide. The picture here is of someone emerging from one of these canyons on to a wide plain.

The psalmist has been restrained, even crushed by slander, persecution, reproach, depression and despair. Now he begins to hope, anticipating that his way will broaden into a wide place. He has been in a narrow valley, but now envisions a new life of freedom.

Everybody wants freedom. Sadly, the freedom the world wants leads only to bondage. To most people freedom means freedom to do as they please. They want the freedom to drink, to use drugs, lie, steal and to have sex with anyone they please. They think a life of obedience to God's Word is a life of bondage, a life filled with thou shall nots. They don't know the difference between lust and liberty. Freedom is a dangerous thing for them. Ask the woman with the unwanted pregnancy. Ask the alcoholic or the man or woman hooked on cocaine. Ask the man or woman behind prison bars or with a sexually trans-mitted disease if they are enjoying the fruits of their freedom to choose their own way.

Eve listened to Satan's lie and exercised her freedom to disobey God and plunged the whole race into bondage. Those who find freedom in God's law are under no restraints or compulsions. They do what they want to do because they want to do only those things which please God. They keep His command-ments and they are not burdensome (I John 1:25).

God's law is called the "perfect law of liberty," by which transgressors will be judged (James 2:12). Jesus said, "If you abide in my word you are my disciples indeed. And you shall know the truth and the truth shall make you free" (John 8:31-32). God's

Word is truth, and only by abiding in it can we be truly free. Solomon described freedom in these words, "When you walk your steps will not be hindered, and when you run you will not stumble" (Prov. 4:12).

Freedom found through the Word doesn't come to the passive, but to those who seek. The word "seek" in this verse means to inquire, study or examine. There is liberating power in searching the Scriptures. Paul said, "Do not be conformed to this world but be transformed by the renewing of your minds" (Rom.12:1). Our minds are renewed by the study of God's Word.

The Word is like water that washes away the filth. It's like a hammer that smashes the strongholds, and like a fire that burns the rubbish. The Word will do these things only if we pursue it persistently and obey it faithfully. Job said, "I have not departed from the commandments of His lips; I have treasured the words of His mouth more than my necessary food" (Job 23:12). It must be with us if we are to walk in liberty!

By Thy law I'm made free.
With it I am agreed,
And by it I now can see.
I am free, free indeed!

B. He Will Talk Fearlessly v. 46

I will speak of Your testimonies also before kings, and will not be ashamed. Perhaps he had been ashamed of God's testimonies before the princes who spoke against him (v.23). But now he will speak fearlessly before kings. We are sometimes intimidated by people in positions of authority, famous people, wealthy people or people we think are smarter than we are. Somehow we think they are different from us. But all are alike in the sight of God. Kings and princes, as well as prostitutes and paupers, are sinners and need a savior.

In verse 45, the psalmist said he would walk in liberty. Timidity might say that his walk before kings would be enough. He might have thought his life and conduct in the royal courts would be a sufficient testimony. Not so! He wanted the boldness to SPEAK to kings about God's Word.

Shadrach, Meshach and Abednego refused to bow down and worship the image of Nebuchadnezzar even if it meant death in the firey furnace. They stood before the king and said, "Our God, whom we serve, is able to deliver us from the burning firey furnace, and He will deliver us from your hand, O king. But, if not, let it be known to you, O king, that we will not serve your gods, nor will we worship the gold image which you have set up" (Dan. 3:17-18).

Standing before the authorities who had forbidden them to teach in the name of Jesus, Peter and John said, "Whether it is right in the sight of God to listen to you more than God, you judge, for we cannot but speak the things which we have seen and heard" (Acts 4:19-20).

Paul spoke boldly of Christ before Felix, Festus and Agrippa. Proverbs 29:25 says, "The fear of man brings a snare, but whoever trust in the Lord shall be safe."

I remember President Ronald Regan speaking before an assembly of communist leaders in China. While explaining the American way of life to the Chinese leaders, he gave a clear presentation of the gospel. He did it boldly without a trace of fear or intimidation.

Paul said, "I am not ashamed of the gospel of Christ for it is the power of God unto salvation" (Rom.1:16). When we speak of God's testimonies we never need to be ashamed. God's grace and power chases shame away.

> Lord, I will speak of Thy name
> To the king upon his throne,
> And tell him without any shame,
> All that Thou hast made known.

IV. ENJOYING THE PLEASURES OF GOD'S WORD VS.47-48

A. He Will Declare His Joy v.47

I will delight myself in Your commandments, which I love. On the meaning of "delight myself" see the comments on verse 16. When he walked in freedom and spoke boldly, the psalmist found delight in God's Word. We don't know whether God's Word delighted those who heard it from him or not, but we do know it delighted him. When we speak the Word of God without fear we will find pleasure in it.

God gives His Word to delight us. Jesus said, "These things I have spoken to you that My joy may remain in you, and that your joy may be full" (John

15:11).The things we delight in and love shape our lives. Where there is no love there is no delight. Again, Jesus said, "If you love Me you will keep my word" (John 14:23). Love is the fulfilling of the law.

Thy Word is my delight.
It's my greatest treasure.
It leads me to the light,
And joy beyond measure.

B. He Will Demonstrate His Joy v.48
  1. Externally v.48a
  My hands I will lift up to Your commandments which I love. The lifting of hands has many meanings in the Old Testament. Translators and commentators differ in regard to what it means here. Most believe it refers to lifting the hands in reverence. Others think it refers to lifting the hands with palms upturned to receive something, like a child extending its hands toward its father with the expectation of a gift.

Either of these would be appropriate, but the meaning that best fits the context here is the idea of lifting the hands in joy and celebration. In the previous verse the psalmist verbally expressed his delight in God's Word. Now he lifts up his hands as physical expression of it.

Lifting the hands is a natural expression of satisfaction and pleasure. Notice how both players and fans raise their hands at baseball games or football games in celebration of outstanding plays and victories by the home team. That's what the psalmist is saying here.

He's promising to celebrate the joy he feels in loving and keeping God's commandments. It's something we often do in church services. When the music brings joy to our hearts, or the preacher points out some thrilling truth, we lift our hands in joy and celebration.

2.   Internally v.48b

And I will meditate on Your statutes. Those who celebrate great victories in sports rehearse them over and over again in their minds and often speak of them to others. The psalmist not only celebrates God's Word, he thinks about it continually. The things we love are always in our thoughts. We think about them night and day. So God's word is always in the Psalmist's thoughts. He rolls the statutes over and over in his mind and longs for more knowledge of them.

My hands are lifted high
To receive Thy commands.
O Lord, for them I cry,
They're all my soul demands.

STANZA 7: PSALM 119:49-56

PRECIOUS MEMORIES

I. Remembering the Promises vs.49-51
  A. Gives Confidence v.49
  B. Gives Comfort vs.50-51
    1. When afflicted v.50
    2. When attacked v.51
II. Remembering the Past vs.53-54
  A. Brings Comfort v.52
  B. Brings Concern v.53
  C. Brings Celebration v.54
III. Remembering the Person vs.55-56
  A. His Name is Remembered v.55
  B. His Nature is Revealed v.56

The psalmist is emerging from darkness and depression. He has found hope in God's Word. Now his hope grows stronger as he remembers. In the last stanza, he looked forward. In this one, he looks back and recalls God's promises and His judgments. These memories encourage him.

This is the only stanza in Psalm 119 in which the verb "remember" appears. In verse 16, he promised not to forget God's Word. Here he remembers it. Memory is a precious gift, and the psalmist has some precious memories.

I. REMEMBERING THE PROMISES
VS.49-51

A. Remembering the Promises Gives Confidence
   v.49
Remember Your word to Your servant, upon which You have caused me to hope. The psalmist asks God to remember His promises. He's not afraid God will forget. He's simply turning God's promise into a prayer. He puts himself into the position of a servant to obey whatever the Lord commands. He didn't say, "Remember my service to You," but "Remember Your Word to me." He asks the Lord to deal with him according to the word He has spoken to him. When we stand on what God has said, we can have great confidence.

The promises of the Bible are usually spoken to all of God's redeemed. But the psalmist treats at least one of them as a personal promise to him. God's promises become real when the Holy Spirit makes them personal to us.

God's promises stir up hope in our hearts. Hope has to do with the future. It looks forward with expectation. It's the seed from which faith springs. Hope isn't just a wish. It's waiting on God with expectation. The Lord will never disappoint the hopes He kindles by His promises, nor will He arouse false hopes within our hearts. "God is not a mere man that He should lie, or the son of man that He should repent. Has He said, and will He not do? Or has He spoken and will not make it good" (Num. 23:19)?

> Remember Thy promises made,
> They fill my every thought.
> With a heart strong and unafraid,
> I cling to the hope they brought.

B. Remembering the Promises Gives Comfort vs.50-51
  1. When afflicted v.50
  This is my comfort in my affliction, For Your word has given me life. The hope he received from God's Word gave the psalmist comfort in time of affliction. We don't know what his affliction was, but he refers to it as "my affliction." So it was something personal. No matter what our affliction, God's Word can bring us hope and comfort. The first place we should go when trouble strikes is to the Bible. Find a promise and hang on to it. God isn't making new promises, but the Holy Spirit can make the promises of the Bible personal to us.

The rich may cling to their wealth and say, "This is my comfort." The drug addict may clinch his drugs and say, "This is my comfort." The alcoholic may hold up his bottle and say, "This is my comfort." But the redeemed can point to the Bible and say, "I find my comfort in this."

God remembers us in our affliction and comforts us. Rachael cried out to the Lord in her barrenness and He remembered her and opened her womb (Gen.30:22). God remembered Isaac and comforted him at his mother's death (Gen. 24:67). Before He returned to heaven Jesus told the 12, "I will not leave you comfortless" (John 14:18).

Paul said, "Blessed be the God and Father of our Lord Jesus Christ, the Father of mercies and the God of all comfort" (II Cor.1:3-4).

Afflictions and trials, especially those that extend over a period of time, can wear us down and drain our strength. God's Word refreshes and restores us. Troubles, which are heavy burdens when we're weak, are only annoyances when we're strong. God's Word gives us hope by its promises, as well as strength to bear life's burdens.

> I trust in Thy Word and no more,
> To comfort me in my afflictions.
> In it I find the strength to soar
> Above trouble's vexing restrictions.

2. When attacked v.51

The proud have me in great derision, yet I do not turn aside from Your law. The word "derision" comes from a word that originally meant "to make a face." Its derived meaning is to scorn, mock or express contempt for someone. The psalmist calls the derision of the proud "great," indicating the intensity and persistence of their scorn. They were cruel with their words and wicked in their schemes, and they never let up.

The arrogant not only boast of their own accomplishments, they mock and discredit the work of those who trust the Lord and live by His Word. When David went out to fight Goliath, the giant mocked him and said, "Am I a dog that you come to me with sticks? I will give your flesh to the birds of the air and the beasts of the field" (I Sam.17:43-44).

When Nehemiah started rebuilding the walls of Jerusalem, Sanballat and Tobiah heard about it and mocked the Jews saying, "Whatever they build, if even a fox goes up on it, he will break down their stone wall" (Neh.4:3).

In Psalm 123:4, another psalmist said, "Our soul is exceedingly filled with the scorn of those who are at ease, with the contempt of the proud." As Christians we can expect to be held in contempt by the proud. They will mock our way of life and minimize the good we do. They will try to discredit God's Word and marginalize our influence.

The proud laughed, but they didn't succeed in turning the psalmist from God's law. He held to it even more firmly. Another psalm says, "All this has come upon us, but we have not forgotten You, nor have we dealt falsely with Your covenant. Our heart has not turned back nor have our steps departed from Your ways" (Ps.44:17-18).

Goliath mocked David, but David didn't turn back and Goliath was defeated. Sanballat and Tobiah mocked Nehemiah and the Jews, but they didn't cease the work and the wall was built. Those who are faithful to the Word of God will always win. God will deal with the proud and the scornful. "Truly, He scorns the scornful, but gives grace to the humble" (Prov. 3:34). When we stand on the Word, the mocking of the proud can't harm us anymore than dogs can harm the moon by howling at it.

> Their mocking I endure.
> I suffer at their hand,
> But in Thee I am secure
> For on Thy law I stand.

II. REMEMBERING THE PAST VS.52-54

A. Remembering the Past Brings Comfort v.52

I remembered Your judgments of old, O Lord, and have comforted myself. In verse 50, the psalmist found comfort by remembering God's promises. Now he finds it in reviewing God's past judgments. God's judgments are His decrees and pronouncements and His righteous acts. His judgments come from both His mouth and His hand. The psalmist is referring to God's judgments of old, meaning from the beginning. They are the judgments recorded in His Word.

A study of God's past judgments reveals that He has always done that which is right. Since God doesn't change, we can be sure He will continue to do right. In Genesis 18:25, God asked Abraham, "Shall not the judge of all the earth do right?"

Justice in man's courts is often distorted by the bias of judges, the prejudices of juries, the skills, or lack thereof, of lawyers, by inadequate information, or by flaws in the laws themselves. But God's judgments are always just.

Israel often forgot God's words and works and had to be reminded of them. "Our fathers in Egypt did not understand Your wonders. They did not remember the multitude of Your mercies"(Ps.106:17). And in Isaiah 46:9, God said, "Remember the former things of old, for I am God and there is no other. I am God and there is none like me."

Anguish focuses our attention on our present situation, and often blurs our memory of the past. When trouble comes we can find comfort by remembering what God has done the past. This seemed to be the case with David in Psalm 77:10-11. "And I said, 'this is my anguish. But I will remember the years of the right hand of the Most High. I will remember the works of the Lord. Surely I will remember Your wonders of old.'"

Paul reminds us, "For whatever things were written before were written for our learning that we, through patience, and comfort of the Scripture, might have hope" (Rom.15:4).

Though mocked and scorned, the psalmist remembered how God had dealt with mockers in the past. "He who sits in the heavens shall laugh; the Lord shall hold them in derision" (Ps.2:4). If we remember how God has bared His holy arm against the haughty and has broken them like a clay pot, their taunts will not trouble us.

It's a great comfort to know the unchanging God who has shown Himself strong on behalf of His people. There is a judge who will avenge His elect in the future just as He has in the past.

> I know Thy judgments of old,
> And according to them it is clear,
> That at a time yet untold,
> The proud will tremble with fear.

B.   Remembering the Past Brings Concern v.53

Indignation has taken hold of me because of the wicked who break Your law. The word indignation implies anger at the wicked. This is probably not a good translation. The King James Version translates it "horror," which may better express the idea. The Hebrew word is *zalaphah*. Its basic meaning is hot wind or burning heat and is used to describe a simoom, a hot violent wind blowing across the desert. It's used in Psalm 11:6 and 5:10 to describe something horrible.

As the psalmist remembers the judgments of the Lord and God's wrath against the wicked, he is horrified. He sees the danger of the wicked in his own time and is greatly troubled.

Today there is almost a total absence of preaching on the wrath of God. So there is little concern about the destiny of the lost. There's no horror over sin because we are taught that no moral judgments should be made concerning the actions of others. If there is no God, there can be no sin against God. All human action is a matter of personal preference.

Unless we are horrified over the coming judgment of the wicked we'll do little to rescue them. If we don't view sin as a terrible transgression against God, there is little reason for repentance. Our moral and spiritual sensitivities are so dulled by our culture we are like Lot who "vexed his soul with the filthy conversation of the wicked" (II Peter 2:7 KJV). Unless we believe people are lost we're not likely to try to find them.

> Those that forsake Thy law
> Walk on a dangerous path.
> With horror their end I saw,
> In the day of Thy great wrath.

C. Remembering the Past Brings Celebration v.54

Your statutes have been my songs in the house of my pilgrimage. Looking back at the judgments of God, the psalmist not only saw things that horrified him, but things that gave him reason to sing. The statutes of God were his song book.

Songs express our longings and our joys. They also lighten our burdens. Paul told the Ephesians to speak to one another "in psalms and hymns and spiritual songs making melody in your hearts to the Lord, giving thanks always for all things to God the Father in the name of our Lord Jesus Christ"(Eph.5:19-20). And James said, "Is any cheerful? Let him sing psalms" (James 5:13).

The psalmist said that the songs he sang were "in the house of his pilgrimage." A pilgrim is one on a journey. From the very first, God's people have been strangers and pilgrims on earth (Heb. 11:13). The Jews on their pilgrimages to Jerusalem for the feasts sang psalms as they traveled. Certain psalms were designated for that purpose.

The psalmist sang the Lord's song in a strange land. The book of the statutes of the Lord was the hymn book of heaven. Every statute was a ballad that reminded him of his heavenly home. He may have lived in an earthly mansion, but it was still a pilgrim's house that paled in comparison to his heavenly home.

Ancient travelers in the East often stopped for the night at an inn where they would join other travelers in singing songs of romance or war. But the psalmist sang the statutes of his God. No matter what his circumstances were, there was always a melody in his heart and a song on his lips. It was the same with Paul and Silas who, with bruised and bloody backs and their feet in stocks, sang praises to God at midnight in the Philippian jail.

> Thy statutes are my song.
> I sing them loud and clear.
> I sing them all day long
> While I'm a pilgrim here.

III. REMEMBERING THE PERSON
VS.55-56

A. His Name is Remembered vs.55

I remember Your name in the night, O Lord, and I keep Your law. Perhaps the psalmist is thinking of a journey where he stopped for the night and remembered the Lord on his bed while others slept. David said, "Meditate within your heart on your bed and be still" (Ps. 4:4). And, "When I remembered You upon my bed, I meditate on You in the night watches" (Ps. 63:6). God's name is a symbol of all He is. To remember it is to recall His character and His attributes.

If His name isn't in our memory, His law will not govern our lives. If we don't think of Him in secret, we won't obey Him openly. Our devotion in the day won't rise above our thoughts in the night. Spurgeon said, "As the actions of the day often create the dreams of the night, so do the thoughts of the night produce the deeds of the day."

In our culture there's an effort to separate morality from God. We want to eliminate the name of God from our schools. Yet we want our children to be good. We substitute slogans for the 10 Commandments and wonder why we have behavior problems among our youth. We have not recognized that we are accountable before God for our actions.

I remember Thee in the night
And think upon Thy ways,
So help me live in Thy light,
The remainder of my days.

B. His Nature is Revealed v.56

This has become mine because I keep Your precepts. What is the "this" he is referring to? We are left to supply the answer. This verse seems to be a summary of the blessings he has received from his good and gracious God. When he remembered

God's name, he is reminded of God's blessings. Despite his afflictions and reproach, he is amazed at all he has received from the hand of his God. God has comforted him in his affliction, strengthened him when the proud scorned him, and gave him joyful songs on his pilgrimage.

All this came to him because he kept God's precepts and found happiness in serving Him. We are again reminded that true happiness comes from God, not from our circumstances. When we obey God's Word in good times and bad, good things will come to us in God's way and in His time. God is good and "He is a rewarder of those who diligently seek Him" (Heb.11:6).

God's best will come to me
When I trust and obey.
In God's time it shall be,
And in His perfect way.

STANZA 8: PSALM 119:57-64

A HIGHER VISION

Introduction v.57a

I. He Reviewed His Past Progress vs.57b-60
    A. What He had Promised v.57b
    B. What He had Prayed v.58
    C. What He had Pondered v.59
    D. What He had Pursued v.60

II. He Resolved His Present Problem vs.61-63
    A. The Problem Stated v.61a
    B. The Problem Solved vs.61b-62
        1. By standing on the Word v.61b
        2. By sincere praise v.62
        3. By supporting friends v.63

III. He Reveals His New Perspective v.64
    A. His Realization v.64a
    B. His Request v.64b

Introduction v.57a

You are my portion O Lord. In Hebrew, this sentence is a broken one without a verb, yet it expresses great joy. The "my portion" may be the "this" of verse 56. If the Lord is his portion he has everything he needs.

God gave each tribe of Israel a portion of the land as an inheritance except for the tribe of Levi. In Numbers 18:20, the Lord told Aaron, "You shall have no inheritance in their land, nor shall you have any portion among them; I am your portion and your inheritance among the children of Israel."

The psalmist saw that having the Lord was better than just having His gifts. Without the Lord he has nothing. To have Him is to have more than anything the world can offer. Others may take his things, but they can never separate him from the Lord. If we lose all our material possessions we still have the Lord as our portion. It is a large and a lasting heritage. It includes all things and outlasts all things. This stanza is the psalmist's response to this realization.

I. HE REVIEWED HIS PAST PROGRESS
VS.57b-60

A. What He had Promised v.57b

I have said I would keep Your words. These words have the strength of a vow. It's the psalmist's natural response to the realization that the Lord is his portion. Jesus said, "If anyone loves me he will keep

My word, and My Father will love him and We will come and make Our home with him" (John 14:23).

John viewed keeping Christ's commandments as proof of knowing Him. "By this we know that we know Him, if we keep His commandments. He who says, 'I know Him,' and does not keep His commandments is a liar and the truth is not in him" (I John 3:3-4). We don't receive salvation by our obedience, but we obey as a result of it. In our obedience we discover the riches of our portion. The more faithful we are the richer our heritage will become.

> The Lord is my portion;
> He meets my every need.
> He's worthy of my devotion
> In every word and deed.

B. What He Had Prayed v.58

I entreated Your favor with my whole heart; be merciful unto me according to Your word. To entreat is to make an appeal or request. The Hebrew word translated "favor" is *panch* which literally means "face." To seek God's face is to seek His presence, and that's how it's translated in Exodus 33:14-15.

When he realized the Lord was his portion, the psalmist wanted to have fellowship with Him and enjoy His favor. God's favor is His face shining upon us. The psalmist is seeking that favor with his whole heart.

The more the psalmist knew about God, the more he felt his need of mercy. The extent that we receive mercy is determined by how much we feel our need. In the parable of the Pharisee and the Publican, the

Pharisee felt no need of mercy. He boasted of his own righteousness but didn't ask for mercy, and he received none. The Publican, on the other hand, felt great need and prayed, "God be merciful to me a sinner," and he received mercy.

The psalmist's request is for mercy to be given to him according to God's Word. His request doesn't go beyond the promises of God's Word, nor does it need to, because sufficient mercy is promised for all our needs and more.

We should note that his cry for mercy is a cry from his heart, not just the mouth. The heart may cry for mercy without the lips, but the cries of the lips that don't come from the heart will never be heard.

Lord, I long to see Thy face.
It's Thy favor I need,
So for Thy mercy and grace,
With my whole heart I plead.

C. What He Had Pondered v.59

I thought about my ways, and turned my feet to Your testimonies. The psalmist's third response to the revelation that the Lord was his portion was to ponder his own behavior. The Hebrew word *chashab* translated "thought" has a wide range of meanings related to thinking. Here it means to give attention to, to closely scrutinize or to consider. It suggests a serious self-examination.

Few of us think at all. Fewer still think on our ways. It's often a painful experience that we prefer to avoid. If we pursue our own ways, without giving careful thought to them, they will lead to sorrow. David's ways led him to adultery and murder. Peter's ways led him to deny Christ. The prodigal's ways led him to the pig pen. Jonah's ways led him to the fish's belly, and Lot's ways led to Sodom.

Too often our thoughts are on what we do or what we have rather than on our ways. The rich fool in Jesus' parable "thought within himself" about his abundant crops and his plans to build bigger barns and enjoy a life of ease, but that night when he stood in the presence of God, none of that mattered.

When the psalmist thought on his ways, he turned his feet to God's testimonies. He changed his thoughts and he changed his walk. Thinking without turning is useless. James compares such a person to a man who looks in a mirror and sees what kind of man he is but goes away and forgets what he looks like. The psalmist first gave attention to his ways then took action to correct them. That's what repentance is. It's a change in mind that results in a change in behavior. Our daily challenge is to consider our ways then line them up with God's Word.

> Lord, I have discerned
> Ways in me not right,
> But now I have turned
> My feet toward the light.

D. What He Had Pursued v.60

I made haste and did not delay to keep Your commandments. The psalmist reflected on his ways, then turned toward God's testimonies. Once he decided he promptly obeyed. He describes his obedience by saying, "I made haste and did not delay." He had a sense of urgency about it. He was in hot pursuit of God's commandments.

We are often quick to sin, but slow to repent and obey. God's timing is perfect. If we are slow to obey we'll miss His best for us. Jonah delayed and he had to pass through the belly of a fish on the road to obedience. Sadly, we sometimes squander days, weeks, months and even years one minute at a time.

Obedience isn't negotiable. When Jesus called Peter, Andrew, James and John, they immediately left their nets and followed Him. Jesus passed by Matthew's tax booth and said, 'Follow Me.' So he arose and followed Him" (Mark 2:14).

These men, like the psalmist, saw the Lord as their portion or inheritance. What He offered them was so valuable that what they left was nothing in comparison. So they didn't hesitate, but obeyed immediately.

Others said they would like to follow Jesus, but wanted to wait until later. One man said, "Let me first go and bury my father." Another said, "I will follow You, but let me first go and bid farewell to those who are at my house." (See Luke 9:59,61) These men hesitated and missed God's appointment, and we never heard from them again.

When I hear Thy command,
I will act, not delay,
And trust that Thy hand
Will lead me each day.

II. HE RESOLVED HIS PRESENT PROBLEM VS.61-63

A. The Problem Stated v.61a

The cords of the wicked have bound me. This statement is an illustration of the imprecise nature of the Hebrew language, especially its poetry. It can be a real problem for translators. The word *hebel* translated "cords" can mean lines, boundary lines, ropes, cords or snares. The Hebrew word for "bound" is *ud* which has a wide range of unrelated meanings depending on the context. It can mean to witness or testify against someone, to admonish, to warn or to surround. The King James Version translates it "robbed." The word is used dozens of times in the Old Testament, but never translated robbed except here. This pictures the psalmist as being tied up and robbed of his possessions. However, that doesn't seem to be the meaning. Most translators prefer the word "surround."

The real meaning might be that the wicked have surrounded him with their snares in the form of false testimony against him. That would be in harmony with verse 23 where he said, "Princes also sit and speak against me." Perhaps their plan was to destroy him by their entrapments in the same way the princes' of Babylon tried to destroy Daniel.

B. The Problem Solved v.61b-63
 1. By standing on the Word v.61b
But I have not forgotten Your law. The wicked may have surrounded him and hemmed him in, but

they couldn't separate the psalmist from the law of God, which was in his heart. He suffered injustice, but it didn't divert his attention from the Word, or diminish his love for it.

God was his portion and the wicked could not deprive him of it, either by force or by falsehood. Many of God's choicest saints through the ages have confirmed that their eternal inheritance in Christ can't be taken away by prison or by death. Like the psalmist, they rested on the promises of the Word of God.

> Snares of the wicked surround me.
> They seek to destroy me with lies,
> But still my heart remains free,
> For Thy Word is before my eyes.

2. By sincere praise v.62

At midnight I will arise and give thanks to You because of Your righteous judgments. The psalmist arose in the middle of the night, not to watch for the wicked or worry about their snares, but to worship. He didn't arise to ponder his problem, but to praise God.

I say his praise was sincere because only sincere people get up in the middle of the night to offer it in secret. He didn't lie in the bed to offer it. He arose to do it. Posture in praise isn't everything, nor is it nothing. There is no virtue in rising and not praising, and there is no sin in praising and not rising. Doing both is better! His rising at midnight to offer praise is the natural response of one who has discovered that God is his portion.

He thanked God because of His righteous judgments. He had read of God's judgments, both declared and demonstrated, concerning justice and injustice. He knew he had been treated unjustly. Yet he thanked God that His righteous judgments would deal with the wicked who surrounded him with their snares.

I raise my voice in the night
Because Thy judgments are just.
They teach me to do the right,
And in them I put my trust.

3. By supportive friends v.63

I am a companion of all who fear You, and of those who keep Your precepts. The psalmist found a solution to his problem, not only by spending his nights with God, but by spending his days with God's people. The companionship and support of God's people is vital for saints who are facing injustice and trials.

The psalmist was a companion of ALL who feared the Lord and kept His precepts. He didn't just hang out with the rich, the powerful and the famous. Those who have the Lord as their portion find instant rapport with all others who have the same inheritance. In traveling to other countries, I've found that there is an immediate bonding with other Christians, even if I don't speak their language, or they mine.

Acts 2:42 tells us that the new believers "continued steadfastly in the apostle's doctrine and fellowship, in the breaking of bread and in prayers." Later when the apostles were arrested and released, "they went to their own companions" (Acts 4:23). Malachi says, "Then those who feared the Lord spoke one to another, and the Lord listened and heard them: So a book of remembrance was written before Him of those who fear the Lord and who meditate on His name" (Mal. 3:16).

The psalmist found pleasure in the company of those who kept the Lord's commandments. He gained strength through their fellowship. He delighted in the company of holy people whether their position in life was humble or high. Some of the most humble of God's saints are among the most treasured.

My friends are friends of God,
Who fear Him and keep His Word.
To some this may seem odd,
For God's truth they've never heard.

III. HE REVEALS HIS NEW PERSPECTIVE V.64

A. His Realization v.64a

The earth, O Lord is full of Your mercy. When the psalmist realized the Lord was his inheritance, he saw the world from a different perspective. He rose above his fellow Israelites who believed God's mercy was contained within the borders of Israel. His higher vision of mercy gave him a new perspective. When his soul was clinging to the dust and his eyes melted in tears, mercy was there. When hemmed in by the snares of the wicked, he was surrounded by God's mercy. God's mercy is wider than the ocean and higher than the sky. God's greatest act of mercy was sending His Son to die on the cross for our sins.

Seeing the earth filled with God's mercy will give us all a new perspective on our own troubles, and the evil times in which we live. Today, some focus only on the evils of the world. It's true that sin is ugly and our culture is crumbling. Still the earth is filled with God's mercy. By it we are blessed. God has withheld His wrath for 2,000 years because He is merciful and not willing that any should perish. Our vision should be on the fact that God's mercy is available to all people everywhere who will call upon the Lord. May it be a call for us all to go into the fields which are ripe and ready for harvest.

B. His Request v.64b

Teach me Your statutes. It's a request the psalmist repeats because the more he knows of his inheritance, the more he wants to know. When he saw the earth filled with God's mercy he longed to know more. The more we know of God's ways the greater our hunger for even more knowledge. Every time we open God's Word, may our prayer be "Lord, extend Your mercy to me and teach me Your statutes."

> Thy mercy fills the sky,
> And plumbs the deepest sea.
> It hears the faintest cry,
> And sets the captives free.

STANZA 9: PSALM 119: 65-72

THE UNIVERSITY OF ADVERSITY

Introduction: v.65 The Psalmist's Blessings
I. The Psalmist is Taught vs. 66-68
    A. The Teaching v.66
        1. The curriculum requested v.66a
        2. The condition required v.66b
    B. The Technique v.67
    C. The Teacher v.68
        1. The teacher's character v.68a
        2. The teacher's conduct v.68b
II. The Psalmist is Tested vs. 69-70
    A. He is Tested by Persecution v.69
    B. He is Tested by Prosperity v. 70
III. The Psalmist is Transformed vs.71-72
    A. By Understanding the Virtue of Suffering v. 71
    B. By Understanding the Value of Scripture v.72

Introduction: v.65

*Y*ou have dealt well with Your servant O Lord, according to Your word. After confessing that the Lord is his portion and that the earth is filled with God's mercy, the psalmist concludes that the Lord has dealt well with him. God always deals well with His children. There are no exceptions. However, we may not think so if we look only at our present circumstances.

Joseph may not have thought so when his brothers sold him as a slave, or when Potiphar threw him into prison, or when the king's butler forgot about him. But in the end, he said to his brothers, "You meant it for evil against me, but God meant it for good" (Gen. 50:20). In all circumstances we must remember "that all things work together for good to those who love God, to those who are the called according to His purpose" (Rom. 8:28).

The work of God's providence is always in harmony with the principles and promises of His Word. The words of His mouth are perfectly balanced with the works of His hands. He doesn't deal with us according to our desires, but according to His plans and purposes for our lives as revealed in His Word. Nothing can happen to us that can't be understood in the light God's Word. That's why Bible study is so important. He deals with us just as He dealt with men and women in the Bible.

This verse gives us the unchanging principles by which God operates His school of affliction.

O Lord, by Thee I am blessed.
Thou hast dealt with me well.
Thy goodness I have confessed,
Thy mercies cease not to tell.

I. THE PSALMIST IS TAUGHT VS.66-68

A. The Teaching v.66
 1. The curriculum requested v.66a

Teach me good judgment and knowledge. The Hebrew word for judgment used here is *taam*. In the physical sense it means taste. It's the ability to distinguish between such things as sweet and sour. Spiritually, it means the ability to discern between good and evil, or wise and foolish. This is one of the things taught in the University of Adversity.

There's a legend about some who wanted to test Solomon's wisdom. They made some artificial flowers so lifelike they couldn't be distinguished for real ones by sight. They put them beside a vase of real flowers across the room from where Solomon was sitting. "Which vase contains the real flowers they asked?"

"Please open the windows," Solomon said. When they did, bees flew in the window and immediately went to the real flowers. Solomon knew that even though he couldn't discern the difference, the bees could.

As we survey the real and the false things in the world, we need the discernment of the bees to tell the difference. There are a lot of fake flowers in the world. They look beautiful, but there's no life in them.

The psalmist wants his spiritual tastes refined to the point where he can distinguish between the fake and the real, even when the fake things are outwardly as attractive as the real.

"Knowledge," as it's used here, refers to knowledge of the truth. It's the kind of knowledge we can acquire by studying the Word. Knowledge and good judgment go together. Without discernment knowledge has little value. Paul said, "And this I pray, that your love may abound still more and more in knowledge and all discernment" (Phil. 1:9).

2. The condition required v.66b

For I believe Your commandments. The prerequisite to learning what God teaches us is a believing heart. This is the basis for acquiring good judgment and knowledge. We can learn nothing from the course if we don't believe the textbook. The Scriptures teach us to understand and interpret the experiences of life. They are a commentary on life. God's Word is not only true, but His commandments are for our good.

The Bible uses words very carefully. Notice that the psalmist doesn't say he believes God's promises, but he believes His commandments. We're to believe and receive God's promises but we're to obey His commandments. Obedience is the key to knowledge and discernment. It gives more insight than study alone. Jesus said, "If anyone wills to do His will, he shall know concerning the doctrine, whether it is from God or whether I speak on my own authority" (John 7:17). If you are not certain about whether the Bible is true or not, obey its commandments and you will know.

Teach me Lord to know
How to choose Thy very best,
So I may in wisdom grow,
And pass life's every test.

B. The Technique v.67

Before I was afflicted I went astray, but now I keep Your word. Affliction is a general word which can refer to any kind of trial. The basic meaning is "to bend or bow down, to humble." It's equivalent to our expression "to bring him to his knees." God used affliction to humble the psalmist and bring him back from his wanderings. It seems that most of our greatest lessons have to be learned through suffering. Even Jesus "learned obedience by the things which He suffered" (Heb. 5:8). Most of the time, we don't learn much from preaching and teaching or even by examples. It takes affliction to get our attention.

We all have "before" and "now" testimonies. Affliction is usually the hinge between the before and the now. Our stories are all different, but the theme is the same. The stories are different because our afflictions are different. For some it's sickness. For others it's persecution, financial problems, family problems, or the loss of loved ones. Sometimes, it may be disappointments and dashed hopes. God, in His wisdom, knows what it will take to humble us before Him and open our hearts to His teaching.

We see an example of God's teaching techniques in II Chronicles 33:10-13. "And the Lord spoke to Manasseh and his people, but they would not listen. Therefore, the Lord brought upon them the captains of the king of Assyria who took Manasseh with hooks, bound him with bronze fetters and carried him off to Babylon. Now when he was in affliction, he implored the Lord his God, and humbled himself greatly before the God of his fathers, and prayed to Him, and He received his entreaty, heard his supplication and brought him back to Jerusalem into his kingdom. Then Manasseh knew that the Lord was God."

However, it's possible to attend the school of affliction and flunk the course. Pharoah did. God sent plague after plague upon Egypt, yet Pharoah continued to harden his heart. Finally, Moses said to him, "How long will you refuse to humble yourself before God" (Ex. 10:3)? He never did.

Israel rebelled against God in the time of the prophet Amos. The Lord sent famine, plagues, pestilence and enemy attacks that destroyed some of their cities, yet they didn't return to the Lord. So the Lord said, "Prepare to meet your God" (Amos 4:6-12).

Affliction alone won't teach us the lessons we need to learn. It's only when the affliction humbles us that we pass the course. Without humility we're unteachable.

A shepherd may sometimes break the leg of a sheep prone to wander from the flock. He does so because he knows if the sheep continues to stray, sooner or later it will be killed by predators. He breaks its leg to save its life. He then carries it upon his shoulders while the leg heals. By the time it heals the sheep will become accustomed to staying with the flock.

I went astray before
I felt Thy afflicting hand.
Now I wander no more,
But on Thy Word I stand.

C. The Teacher v.68

1. The teacher's character v.68a

You are good. God is the essence of goodness. Jesus told the rich young ruler, "No one is good but one, that is God." (Luke 18:19). His goodness is like an ocean without bottom or shore. It's said of some teachers that their courses are hard, but they are fair. God's courses may be hard and His methods painful, but He is good. "O give thanks unto the Lord for He is good" (Psalm 107:1).

2. The teacher's conduct v.68b

And do good. God acts according to His nature. His goodness is not passive good. What God is, God does. Jesus, who was the incarnation of God's nature, went about doing good. As God's children, and partakers of His nature, we are to manifest His good works that others may see them and glorify Him. As students in the University of Adversity, we learn to be like our teacher.

If God is good, and does good, then His statutes are good. They reflect His good character and His good deeds. It's always an advantage to the students if the teacher has written the textbook.

Thy goodness overwhelms me,
Like a sea without bottom or shore,
My heart I open to Thee,
For I want to know more and more.

II. THE PSALMIST IS TESTED VS.69-70

A. He is Tested by Persecution v.69

The proud have forged a lie against me but I will keep Your precepts with my whole heart. We have met the proud before (v.31). The psalmist suffered many afflictions, but those he mentioned most are the slanders and lies spoken against him by the proud. The Hebrew word *tapal* translated "forged" means to plaster over or patch together. It refers to conducting a smear campaign against someone so that the truth is completely covered over with lies. Zemek translates it, "Indolent men have plastered falsehood over me." It suggests gathering various words taken out of context and patching them together into a story that might be believable, but entirely untrue.

It's hard to combat this kind of lie because the liars patch together our own words to create the lie. Jesus was the victim of forged lies. One of the witnesses at His so-called trial testified that Jesus said if you tear down the temple He would rebuild it in three days. Did Jesus say that? Yes, but He was referring to His death and resurrection, not to the Jewish temple.

It's the kind of lies politicians and the media forge. The psalmist is put to the test by these forgers of lies, but he passes the test. Their lies won't provoke him to defend himself or divert him from God's Word.

Instead, they drove him to seek and obey God's precepts with his whole heart.

If you've ever had lies forged against you know that what the psalmist did required great discipline. If we try to answer lies we may lose the battle, but we can have victory through faithful obedience to God's precepts.

> When about me lies are told
> By the arrogant and the proud,
> I recall Thy precepts of old,
> And to keep them I have vowed.

B. He is Tested by Prosperity v.70

Their heart is as fat as grease, but I delight in Your laws. The proud have grown prosperous and insensitive. Their hearts have grown so fat by their self-indulgent living that they're impervious to the truth. You might wonder why I consider their condition a test for the psalmist.

The picture of the proud and prosperous living a life of ease is a temptation to the righteous who are afflicted. The author of Psalm 73 writes about it.

> But as for me, my feet almost stumbled. My steps nearly slipped, for I was envious of the boastful, when I saw the prosperity of the wicked... Their eyes bulge with abundance. They have more than heart could wish. ... Behold, these are the ungodly who are always at ease. They increase in riches. Surely I have cleansed my heart in vain and washed my

hands in innocence. For all day long I have been plagued and chastened every morning When I thought how to understand this it was too painful for me until I went into the sanctuary of God and saw their end. Surely You set them in slippery places. You cast them down to destruction (Ps. 73:2-18).

We are constantly tempted by the lure of the lifestyles of the rich and famous as portrayed by the media. When we see the cars they drive, the houses they live in, the clothes they wear and the places they go, it's hard to be content with what we have. Unfortunately, even some ministers have yielded to this temptation. Paul said, "Those who want to be rich fall into temptation and a snare, and into many harmful lusts" (I Tim. 6:9).

The psalmist passed the test. He finds his delight in God's law rather than in the luxuries of the rich. Our delights are an index of our characters. When God's Word is our delight we become sensitive and teachable. When we delight in worldly possessions and pleasures we become spiritually dull and stupid.

While the ungodly are at ease
And their hearts fat with pleasure,
I open God's Word on my knees
And find joy without measure.

III. THE PSALMIST IS TRANSFORMED
VS. 71-72

A. By Understanding the Virtue of Suffering v.71

It is good for me that I have been afflicted, that I may learn Your statutes. The psalmist now rises to a new level. He has said before that God was good and His law was good. Now he says that God's afflictions are also good. He has mentioned them, prayed about them, but only now does he see that they are good. This is a transforming insight.

His afflictions seem to have come from bad men, but still they are good. Some of our afflictions come from evil people, some come from the devil and some are God's chastening. Others we bring on ourselves. Whatever their source, God can use them for good. Good doesn't always mean pleasant. Sometimes it's very unpleasant. We have reached an important level in our lives when we can say, "It was good for me that I have been afflicted."

Affliction not only leads us to God's Word, it helps us to understand it. The psalmist seems to be saying affliction is a qualification for learning God's statutes. Whatever leads us to the Word, and helps us understand it, is good. So let us thank God for our afflictions. "In everything give thanks, for this is the will of God in Christ Jesus for you" (I Thess. 5:18).

I have preached and taught God's Word for nearly 60 years, but I'm still enrolled in the University of Adversity.

Thy dealings with me are good,
Even though they bring pain.
I'd not change them if I could,
For they have brought great gain.

B. By His Understanding of the Value of Scripture
v.72

The law of Your mouth is better to me than thou-sands of coins of gold and silver. The psalmist learned the true value of things in the school of affliction. The Word is the law of God's mouth. It was just as fresh and powerful to the psalmist as if God had just been whispered in his ear. Words that come from the lips of the heavenly Father are highly prized.

"Thousands of coins of gold and silver," suggests an unlimited amount. Gold and silver are mined from the earth which God created by His Word. Is the creator of the gold and silver not of greater value than His coins? "Receive my instruction and not silver, and knowledge rather than choice gold. For wisdom is better than rubies and all the things one may desire cannot be compared to her" (Prov.8:10-11).

If you're foolish the law can make you wise, but money can only make you a rich fool. God's Word can give you comfort when you come to die. Riches can only give you a good funeral.

The University of Adversity teaches us the differ-ence between the temporary treasures of the world and the eternal values of heaven. Paul said, "For our light affliction, which is but for a moment, is working for us a far more exceeding and eternal weight in glory. While we do not look at the things which are seen, but at the things which are not seen. For the things which are seen are temporary, but the things which are not seen are eternal" (II Cor. 4:17-18).

O Lord, Thy words I prize.
They are of measureless worth.
Obeying them makes me wise
With wisdom far above this earth.

PREPARING FOR THE NEXT STEP

I. The Psalmist's Perspective vs. 73-75
   A. On the Making of His Life v.73
   B. On the Meaning of His Life v.74
   C. On the Molding of His Life v.75
II. The Psalmist's Prayer vs. 76-80
   A. For Sure Comfort vs. 76-77
      1. From God's covenant v.76
      2. From God's compassion v.77
   B. For Supportive Companions vs. 78-79
      1. The companions he rejected v. 78
      2. The companions he required v.79
   C. For Sound Counsel v.80

In the last stanza the psalmist struggled through the painful courses in the University of Adversity.

Now he looks at his life, reviews what he has learned and asks God to meet his needs as he goes forward.

I. THE PSALMIST'S PERSPECTIVE VS. 73-75

A. On the Making of His Life v.73

Your hands have made me and fashioned me; give me understanding that I may keep Your commandments. The doctrine of creation is the fundamental doctrine of the Bible. If man evolved out of a slime pit we are no better than the other animals that emerged out of the slime with us. We are not accountable to God, so there is no sin and no redemption from sin. God is a myth and the Bible is a lie. If we are the product of chance, nothing we believe is true and nothing we do matters.

Serial killer Jeffery Dahmer said, in an interview with Stone Phillips on NBC, that his belief in evolution was partly responsible for his murdering 17 men and boys between 1978 and 1991.

"I didn't feel accountable to anyone. I didn't feel I would have to ever face what I had done. I always believed the lie that evolution was truth, that we all just came from slime, and when we die, that's it," he said. "Then I started reading books that show how that evolution is a complete lie. There's no basis in science to support it. I've since come to believe that the Lord Jesus Christ is the true creator of the heavens and the earth. It just didn't happen. And I have accepted Him as my Lord and Savior. I believe that I, as well as everyone else, will be accountable to Him."

Of course, not everyone who believes in evolution will become a serial killer, but men and women who believe they are not accountable to God for their actions will do things they would not otherwise do. If Genesis is not true, Matthew, Mark, Luke and John are irrelevant.

The psalmist declares that God made us with His hands. We are hand crafted. God created Adam out of the dust, and each of us through the reproductive powers He gave to Adam. The Bible affirms the doctrine of divine creation again and again. Job said, "Your hands have made me and fashioned me, an intricate unity" (Job 10:8). And in Psalm 139:13-14, "For You formed my inward parts, You covered me in my mother's womb. I will praise You for I am fearfully and wonderfully made."

God's handiwork is very evident in the intricacies of our minds and bodies. Think of the intricate circulatory system and the life-giving blood pumped through the miles of blood vessels by the heart at the rate of 2,500 gallons per day. Or consider the brain, more powerful than the most powerful computer, making continuous calculations as it receives and sends out millions of messages through a complex network of nerves. How about the eyes, the photographic equipment which takes three-dimensioned action shots and colored pictures? The digestive system, the reproductive system and the respiratory system, all testify that God made us by His hand. I don't have enough faith to believe all this happened by chance.

The psalmist says God not only made him, but "fashioned" him. Again he uses the Hebrew *kun*, translated "fashioned," which means to constitute, make ready or prepare. For example, it's used to describe adjusting a weapon for a target. God not only created us, but also prepared each of us for His specific purpose. He prepared us by giving us gifts and abilities to fulfill that purpose.

Since God has created and fashioned him, the psalmist asks for an understanding of His commandments. If He made us, surely He will help us understand the manufacturer's manual so we can fulfill His purpose for us.

Thou alone hast made me;
Fashioned me to do Thy will.
So help me to know Thee,
And Thy purpose to fulfill.

B. On the Meaning of his Life v.74

They who fear You shall be glad when they see me because I have hoped in Your word. The psalmist didn't find meaning in life by hiding in a cave and reading his Bible. He found it in bringing gladness to all who fear the Lord. The word "glad" comes from a word used to describe the cheer wine brings, the pleasant smell of perfume and the joy a wise son brings to his father. Our lives become meaningful to the extent that we reach out to others to cheer and comfort them. When we do, those who fear the Lord will be glad to see us.

The psalmist passed gladness along to his God-fearing friends because of his hope in God's Word which told him he had been made and fashioned for God's purpose. If God didn't create us and fashion us, life is meaningless. Those who understand their origin and purpose will bless the lives of those around them.

Evolutionists and atheists don't bring comfort and cheer to anyone because they have no hope and their lives have no meaning. We don't call on them for comfort when afflicted or counsel when we face death because they have neither counsel nor comfort to give.

The hope of the lost is like a mirage on the desert. It's an illusion that promises much but brings only disappointment and death. The believer, on the other hand, finds meaning in sharing God's Word to cheer and comfort his fellow travelers along the way.

> Those who walk in Thy fear
> Will look to me and be glad,
> As I seek their hearts to cheer,
> That to their hope I may add.

C. On the Molding of his Life v. 75
I know O Lord, that Your judgments are right, and in faithfulness You have afflicted me. The psalmist has learned his lessons well in the school of affliction. God's judgments are right, both in what they do and what they declare. The judgments of His hand are for

our correction, and the judgments of His mouth are for our instruction. They are right in what they reveal and in what they require. God orders all things and He orders them correctly. He is fair in what He gives and in what He takes away.

"He is the Rock. His work is perfect, for all His ways are justice, a God of truth and without injustice; Righteous and upright is He" (Deut. 32:4). Job said, "Surely God will never do wickedly, nor will the Almighty pervert justice" (Job 34:12).

We try to correct our children in order to mold their lives in the right way. At times we may over react or under react. We may be unfair, but God never is. His corrections are always appropriate. He is faithful in always doing right and doing it in the proper way. His chastening is always administered in perfect balance between what is right and what is appropriate.

> Lord, all Thy judgments are just,
> And Thy ways are fair.
> So in Thy faithfulness I trust.
> Thy goodness I declare

II. THE PSALMIST'S PRAYER VS.76-80

A. For Sure Comfort vs. 76-77
  1. From God's covenant v.76
Let, I pray, Your merciful kindness be for my comfort, according to Your word to Your servant. "Merciful kindness" is the translation of the Hebrew word *hesed,* a covenant word, and one of the most

important words in the Old Testament. It embraces the character of God as revealed in His covenants with His people. It's used 26 times in Psalm 136 to proclaim God's kindness and eternal love. God's merciful kindness is the foundation for His faithfulness.

The psalmist's prayer for comfort is deeply rooted in the character of God. It's not based on his feelings, but on God's promises. He's seeking comfort from the same hand that made him and fashioned him. He doesn't pray that his afflictions be removed, only that he be comforted in them.

"The Lord is merciful and gracious, slow to anger and abounding in mercy. He will not always strive with us, nor will He keep His anger forever. He has not dealt with us according to our sins, nor punished us according to our iniquities. For as the heavens are high above the earth, so great is His mercy toward them that fear Him" (Ps.103:8-11). The psalmist has already seen that the earth is filled with God's mercy (v.64), now he relies on it for comfort.

With the words, "for MY comfort," he makes God's general promise of mercy his personal promise. The general delivery promise now has his name on it. Sometimes the Holy Spirit makes a general promise personal to us.

The idea of the personal promise to the psalmist is confirmed by the words, "according to Your words to Your servant." These are words spoken by God to him, and for him. They calm his fears, sooth his anxieties and comfort him in his affliction.

In need of Thy mercy I stand,
May Thy kindness come to me
And the comfort of Thy hand.
According to Thy Word, let it be.

2. From God's compassion v.77

Let Your tender mercies come to me that I might live, for Your law is my delight. The words "tender mercies" are from the Hebrew word *raham*, meaning compassion, pity or tender affections. Zemek says it refers to a deep love, such as a mother's love for a baby, or a father's love for his son. It's often connected with love for helpless people.

In addition to the merciful kindness related to God's covenant faithfulness, the psalmist finds comfort in God's compassionate heart, which is above and beyond His covenant mercies. So this is not just a repetition of his request in verse 76, but an extension of it.

In verse 76 he asks for mercy to comfort him. Now he asks for multiple mercies that he might live. We don't know if he means that his life is threatened, or it's so limited by his circumstances that he's not really living. In either case, he needs God's mercy.

Many who have suffered affliction have asked for justice. However, what we really need is mercy, not justice. My lifelong friend, Ron Dunn, now with the Lord, was a widely known Bible teacher. He said he once went to a photographer to have some publicity pictures made. After looking at the pictures, he told the photographer that the pictures didn't do him justice. The photographer replied, "Brother Ron, you don't need justice, you need mercy." That's true of us all, especially in the light of the penetrating photography of God.

David spoke of God "who redeems your life from destruction, who crowns you with lovingkindness and tender mercies" (Ps. 103:4). James spoke of the Lord as "very compassionate and merciful" (James 5:11).

The psalmist's appeal isn't based on his own merit, but on his delight in God's law. He delighted in it when it corrected him and when it comforted him, when he was grieving and when he was glad, when he was poor and when he was prosperous. Our pleas for mercy must always be based on the promises of God's Word, never on our own goodness or works.

Lord, Let thy mercies come,
That I might continue to live.
Let my enemies be dumb,
And I will praises to Thee give.

B. For Supportive Companions vs.78-79
  1. The companions he rejected. v.78
  Let the proud be ashamed for they treat me wrongly with falsehood, but I will meditate on Your precepts. The psalmist rejected the companionship of the proud. He had no part with them. They were a perpetual plague to him. We've met them before, and we'll meet them again. Sometimes he calls them the proud and sometimes the wicked. They are the same. He doesn't pray that they'll be destroyed, only that

they'll be ashamed. He's asking that they'll be embar-
rassed by the failure of their plots against him.

The African lion is called the king of the jungle,
primarily because of its ability to intimidate the other
animals with its deafening roar. Native hunters stand
completely still when the lion roars. When the hunters
don't move, the lion gets confused. The hunters then
take advantage of the confusion and close in for the
kill.

The psalmist refuses to be intimidated by the lies
of the proud. He knows that, in the end, they will
become confused and fail. Pride carries the seeds of
its own destruction. "A man's pride will bring him
low, but the humble in spirit will retain his honor"
(Prov. 29:23).

The psalmist isn't asking for revenge. He's
placing the proud in God's hands because he knows
He will bring them down in His own time. Paul said,
"Beloved, do not avenge yourselves, but rather give
place to wrath; for is written, 'vengeance is mine. I
will repay,' says the Lord" (Rom.12:19). That's what
the psalmist is doing.

He knows the worst thing he can do is to allow
their attacks to divert his attention from God's Word.
He didn't waste his time devising ways to retaliate.
Instead, he chose to meditate on God's precepts. That
was the best way to confound them.

> The proud are put to shame,
> Crushed beneath their lies,
> But I'll call upon Thy name
> As I wait for their demise.

2. The companions he required v.79

Let those who fear You turn to me, those who know Your testimonies. The psalmist prays for companions who fear the Lord. His name may be cast out as evil by the proud, but he wants the companionship of God's people. Friendships based on earthly things, like wealth, occupations, position, class or rank, are temporary. But the friendships among God's people are eternal because the basis of their friendships never ends.

He asked the Lord for friends who feared the Lord, and who knew His testimonies. When people who fear the Lord and love His Word get together, there's a sound basis for friendship. Spurgeon said, "When fearing and knowing walk hand in hand they cause us to be thoroughly furnished unto every good work." May we all seek to be numbered among those who both fear God and know His testimonies.

> For friends my heart is yearning,
> Friends who fear Thy name,
> Friends who are always learning,
> Who love without blame.

C. For Sound Counsel v.80

Let my heart be blameless regarding Your statutes, that I may not be ashamed. The word "blameless" is the same word translated undefiled in verse 1. It means complete or whole. It's translated "sound" in the KJV. The psalmist takes his counsel from the statutes of God which are perfect and complete, and he wants his heart to be the same way in regard to God's statutes.

We have all been victims of bad counsel at one time or another – bad financial counsel, bad legal counsel, bad family counsel or bad spiritual counsel. The worst counsel of all comes from our own defiled and divided hearts. The only perfect counsel is that which comes from God's pure Word to a pure heart.

Those who listen to the counsel of God's Word, and live by it, will never have reason to be ashamed. It's only when we disobey God's Word that we bring shame upon ourselves.

> Let my heart be blameless and pure,
> As I study Thy perfect law,
> Then Thy counsel to me will insure
> That my ways are without flaw.

A CRY FROM THE DARKNESS

I. The Psalmist's Condition vs.81-83
   A. His Fainting Soul v.81
   B. His Failing Eyes v.82
   C. His Furrowed Face v.83
II. The Psalmist's Complaints vs.84-87
   A. About the Delays v.84
   B. About the Deceivers v.85
   C. About the Dangers vs. 86-87
      1. His persecutors v.86
      2. His peril v.87
III. The Psalmist's Cry v.88
   A. His Plea v.88a
   B. His Promise v.88b

Spurgeon says that this stanza is the midnight of the 119th Psalm. The sky is dark yet the stars are shining and verse 88 gives promise of the dawn. It's the middle stanza of the psalm and the psalmist is in great darkness, He doesn't ask if, or what or why, only when. When will it all be over? When will the morning come? When will he be comforted? When will justice come?

I. THE PSALMIST'S CONDITION VS. 81-83

A. His Fainting Soul v.81

My soul faints for Your salvation, but I hope in Your word. You've probably seen movies where it seems like things can't get worse, but they do. The hero is pushed to the point of desperation just before he wins the game and gets the girl.

The psalmist is completely exhausted, and utterly consumed by trouble. He has nothing to hold to except the Word of God. He's at the end of his rope. Only hope sustains him. He is helpless but hopeful. David said, "I would have lost heart unless I had believed that I would see the goodness of the Lord in the land of the living. Wait on the Lord. Be of good courage and He shall strengthen your heart. Wait, I say upon the Lord" (Ps. 27:13-14). Also, "My flesh and my heart fail; but God is the strength of my heart and my portion forever" (Ps. 73:26).

The psalmist's hope for deliverance is based firmly on God's Word. He's not trying to devise some deliverance of his own. Satan tries to divert us to his solutions to our problems. One of the temptations of Jesus was to satisfy His hunger by turning stones into bread. When we accept the devil's solutions to our problems, we give him authority over us. Jesus refused all compromise. "Consider Him who endured such hostility from sinners against Himself, lest you become weary and discouraged in your souls" (Heb. 12:3).

Abraham grew tired of waiting and took Sarah's sinful suggestion that he have a child with Hagar, her handmaid. Ishmael was born, and the world is still suffering the consequences.

> Lord, all my strength is gone,
> Yet I'm holding to Thy Word,
> From which my hope is drawn.
> And my yearning heart is stirred.

B. His Failing Eyes v.82

My eyes fail from searching Your word, saying, "When will You comfort me?" In verse 81, he hopes for God's deliverance, but it doesn't come. In this verse, he searches God's Word for comfort while he waits, but he can't find it. The reference to his eyes failing may mean he has read the Word until his eyes are blurred. More likely, it's a poetic expression meaning he is yearning for something he can't find. Or maybe it's an unfulfilled expectation, like looking for a letter day after day that never arrives. Proverbs 13:12 says, "Hope deferred makes the heart sick, but when the desire comes, it is a tree of life."

He's asking the questions that Aspah asked in Psalm 77:7-9. "Will the Lord cast off forever? And will He be favorable no more? Has His mercy ceased forever? Has His promise failed forevermore? Has God forgotten to be gracious? Has He in anger shut up His tender mercies?"

When sight fails, faith still sees. "Faith is the substance of things hoped for, the evidence of things not seen" (Heb. 11:1). Paul said, "While we do not look at the things which are seen, but the things which are not seen, for the things which are seen are temporary, but the things which are not seen are eternal" (II Cor, 4:18).

God is never late with His comfort and deliverances, but sometimes our expectations are early.

From looking my eyes are blurred.
Still no comfort can I find.
All my cries have gone unheard
And my pleas are declined.

C. His Furrowed Face v.83

For I have become like a wineskin in smoke, yet I do not forget Your statutes. In the Middle East during Bible times, bottles for water and wine were made out of skins. When empty they were hung inside the tents where smoke and heat from the open fires blackened and cracked them. The psalmist felt like one of these shriveled wineskins ready to be discarded. Perhaps his prolonged sorrow had actually altered his appearance and made him unattractive as it did Job.

At the height of his affliction for our sins, Jesus' appearance was altered by His suffering. The prophecy of this is depicted in Psalm 22. And Isaiah said of Him, "...So His visage was marred more than any man, and His form more than the sons of men" (Isa. 52:14).

The psalmist may have been wrinkled, dry and shriveled, and ready to be thrown on the ash heap, but he holds firmly to God's Word. He doesn't give up his faith. The worst of circumstances can't separate a true believer from his faith. Even when he finds no comfort in it, he still believes God's Word.

There's a great spiritual lesson in this verse for us all. Only when we feel useless can God use us. The old nature is useless to God. Jesus illustrated this when He said, "Nor do they put new wine in old wineskins, or else they would break, the wine is spilled and the wineskins are ruined. But they put new wine in new wineskins and both are preserved" (Matt.9:14). Our old nature can't hold the new life which we receive so it must be brought to the end of itself before we can become useful.

Paul always seemed to face circumstances that were beyond his human ability. However, it was in these circumstances that he was most useful to God. He said, "But we have this treasure in earthen vessels, that the excellence of the power may be of God and not of us. We are hard-pressed on very side, yet not crushed. We are perplexed, but not in despair; persecuted, but not forsaken; struck down, but not destroyed – always carrying about in the body the dying of the Lord Jesus, that the life of Jesus may also be manifested in our body"(II Cor. 4:7-10).

It's through our brokenness that we are able to minister the life of the Spirit to others.

I'm like a wineskin in the smoke,
Ready to be cast away.
Judged by the wicked a joke,
Yet Thy Word I still obey.

II. THE PSALMIST'S COMPLAINTS VS. 84-87

A. About the Delays v.84

How many are the days of Your servant? When will You execute judgment on those who persecute me? The psalmist feels his time is short. Unless the Lord delivers him soon his burden will crush the life from him. He feels as David did in Psalm 39:4-5, "Lord, make me to know my end, and what is the measure of my days, that I may know how frail I am. Indeed, You have made my days as a handbreadth, and my age is nothing before You; certainly every man at his best state is but a vapor."

Long life may seem a calamity rather than a blessing for some. It may seem that our burdens increase as our strength decreases. The days of our lives may seem long because our burdens are heavy. We may pray for relief from our burdens, even if it means death.

Several people in the Bible help us understand God's strange delays and see His wise plan for our lives. Job questioned God in his suffering, as did Jeremiah. Joseph certainly wondered why he was falsely accused and thrown into prison. Our perspectives are too limited for us to see how God is working out His plan in our lives.

The psalmist's question was not, "will You execute judgment?" but, "when will You execute judgment?" He knows God's judgment is sure, but he wonders if he will live long enough to see it. He wants to see his name cleared and his persecutors silenced while he still lives.

Vengeance is the Lord's. He will execute it in His own time, not ours.

My days are near an end,
I may not long survive.
Wilt Thou my life extend,
Til Thy judgments arrive?

B. About the Deceivers v.85

The proud have dug pits for me, which are not according to Your law. The psalmist's enemies are relentless in trying to destroy him. Their slander and lies were not enough. Now they set traps for him.

God never tries to trap us. Only the devil resorts to traps. In the Old Testament, men could dig pits to trap wild animals, but if a tame animal fell into one of them, the man who dug the pit had to reimburse the animal's owner (See Ex. 21:33-34) The proud were unlawfully trying to trap the psalmist like a wild animal.

The metaphor of the pit illustrates the traps of many kinds which his enemies had designed to trap him, just as Daniel's enemies set traps for him, and Jesus' enemies tried to ensnare Him.

Those who dig pits for others are often the ones who fall into them. "He who digs a pit will fall into it" (Eccl. 10:18). And, "He made a pit and dug it out and has fallen into the pit which he made" (Ps. 7:15). Again, "They have dug a pit before me, into the midst of it they themselves have fallen" (Ps.57:6). Remember how Haman prepared a gallows for hanging Mordecai, but was hanged on it himself (See Esther 7:10). History is filled with examples of the wicked meeting the same fate they planned for others.

Knowing the proud were setting traps for him kept the psalmist on high alert. It made him more careful to avoid falling into their pits. The devil never ceases to dig pits for us, so we should always be alert to his devices.

> They have dug pits for me,
> And plotted my demise.
> Their own sin they don't see,
> As new evils they devise.

C. About the Dangers v.86-87
　1. His persecutors v.86
　All Your commandments are faithful. They perse-cute me wrongfully. Help me! In this verse we see the psalmist's praise, his problem and his prayer. He praises God for His commandments because they are faithful. That is, they can be relied upon and trusted. Obeying the commandments might be rough, but it is right. It might make him enemies, but God will be his friend.

His problem was that his enemies persecuted him wrongfully. Their hostility was without cause.

He is like a man sentenced to prison for a crime he didn't commit. He contrasts the faithfulness of God's commandments with the injustice he is receiving at the hands of men.

We can expect such injustice if we are true followers of Christ. Jesus said, "A servant is not greater than his master. If they persecuted me, they will also persecute you" (John 15:20). Paul said, "And all who desire to live godly in Christ Jesus will suffer persecution" (II Tim.3:12).

His prayer was one of few words but full of meaning. It was a prayer of desperation. A drowning man doesn't pray a long prayer filled with flowery words. "Help me", is the prayer Peter prayed as he began to sink beneath the waves (Matt.14:30). It's the prayer millions have prayed. It's appropriate in any situation of desperate need. It's suitable for the young as well as the old. God's help is our hope. No other help is sufficient for our needs. It's the impulsive cry of every child of God.

> Thy Word is faithful and true.
> On it I can rely,
> And no matter what others do,
> Still to Thee I cry.

2. His peril v.87

They almost made an end of me on earth, but I did not forsake Your precepts. "Made an end of" is a translation of the Hebrew word *kaiah*, which means to finish or complete something. We might say today that they almost wiped him out, or demolished him so that nothing was left. His life is in great peril. Their persecution was so severe and so long that his strength was exhausted and he was ready to die.

However, their destruction was only an earthly destruction. They could put his body in the grave, but they couldn't destroy his soul. Jesus said, "Do not fear those who kill the body but cannot kill the soul. But rather fear Him who is able to destroy both body and soul in hell" (Matt. 10:28).

The psalmist was almost destroyed, but not quite. He had escaped by the skin of his teeth. The lions can roar, but they are chained and can come only as far as God permits. The devil was permitted to take away Job's possessions, his children and his health, but he couldn't touch his life.

Neither fear nor pain nor loss could shake the psalmist from God's Word. He believed that if he stuck with the precepts he would be rescued by the promises. He's willing to lose everything, even his life, rather than abandon God's Word. The more his enemies lied about him, slandered him and dug pits for him, the tighter he held to God's Word. He never resorts to revenge. He just clings to the Word, and leaves vengeance to his God.

I'm almost destroyed, but not quite,
By those who want me to fail.
I will always do what is right.
By Thy Word I will prevail.

III. THE PSALMIST'S CRY V.88

A. His Plea v.88a

Revive me according to Your lovingkindness. Nine times in Psalm 119, the psalmist cries out for God to revive him. He has been hammered by his persecutors until his life is nearly beaten out of him. He is down but not out. He is depressed, but not defeated. His plea is that God will recharge his batteries and revive his life force and renew his energy. He doesn't ask that his affliction be removed, only that he will have the strength to bear it.

His plea is based on God's lovingkindness, not on his own goodness. As we have noted before, lovingkindness is from the Hebrew word *hesed,* a powerful covenant word. His only hope is in God's grace. So is ours!

B. His Promise v.88b

So that I might keep the testimony of Your mouth. None of us can keep the testimony of God's mouth unless He gives us the strength to do it. So the psalmist asks for the strength to keep God's Word.

It isn't in our power to arrange the circumstances of our lives in a way that will make life easy. It's our responsibility to obey God's Word in all our circumstances. That's what the psalmist promised to do.

New life from Thee I desire,
So hear now my request.
To keep Thy Word I aspire,
And give to Thee my best.

STANZA 12: PSALM 119:89-96

GOD'S FAITHFUL WORD

I. The Revelation of God's Faithful Word vs. 89-91
    A. Its Faithfulness is Proclaimed v.89
    B. Its Faithfulness is Promised v.90
    C. Its Faithfulness is Proven v.91
II. The Review of God's Faithful Word vs.92-93
    A. It Brought the Psalmist Rejoicing v.92
    B. It Brought the Psalmist Revival v.93
III. The Response to God's Faithful Word vs.94-96
    A. The Psalmist Pursued God's Word v.94
    B. The Psalmist Perused God's Word v.95
    C. The Psalmist Proclaimed God's Word v.96

The psalmist is revived in answer to his plea in verse 88. He now stands on higher ground and receives a new understanding of God and His faithful

Word. He loves the Word even more and clings to it even tighter.

I. THE REVELATION OF GOD'S FAITHFUL WORD VS.89-91

A. Its Faithfulness is Proclaimed v.89

Forever, O Lord, Your word is settled in heaven. The Hebrew word for settled is *nasab,* which means to place or set up and let stand. It's used to describe the stability of alters, columns, and monuments. God has spoken and what He has said stands firm continually. Time will never diminish or alter it. The psalmist will refer to the firmness of God's Word again in verse 152.

Isaiah said, "The grass withers and the flower fades, but the word of our God stands forever" (Isa. 40:8). Jesus said, "Heaven and earth shall pass away, but My words will by no means pass away" (Matt. 24:35).

What God has declared true will always be true. What He has declared to be right will always be right, and what He has declared to be wrong will always be wrong. What He has said is not subject to the opinions of men. It remains absolute truth no matter how many so called scholars declare it to be a book of myths and legends, and no matter how many polls show that a large percentage of people no longer believe it to be absolute truth.

Voltaire said, as he held up a Bible, "In 50 years I will have this book in the morgue." Fifty years later Voltaire was in the morgue and French Bible Society owned his house and used it as a warehouse to store Bibles.

God's Word is settled in heaven in contrast to the unsettled conditions on earth. When our own thoughts and lives are unsettled, we can find comfort in God's Word. May it be as settled in our hearts as it is in heaven. These words seemed to burst from the psalmist's pen as words of praise. Let us join him in praise to God for His settled Word!

Thy Word in heaven is fixed,
Spoken in eternity past,
Thy truth with error unmixed
Will all creation outlast.

B. Its Faithfulness is Promised v.90

Your faithfulness endures to all generations; You have established the earth, and it abides. God's promises were made in ancient times yet they are not worn out or weakened by the passing of the years. They were as true for the psalmist as they were for Abraham, Isaac and Jacob. And they are just as true for us today. The centuries run their weary rounds, and nations flourish and fall, but God's promises still endure.

Not only is God's Word true and His promises valid for all generations, but He has preserved it century after century despite man's efforts to corrupt it and destroy it.

God "established" the earth. The Hebrew word is *kun* the same word use in verse 73 to describe how God "fashioned" us and made us ready or prepared us for a specific purpose. God not only created the earth, He designed it and crafted it for us to live. He prepared the laws of nature to keep it running until His purpose is accomplished. All science is predicated on the fact that God's laws do not change.

If the earth was closer to the sun, we would burn up. If it was farther away, we would freeze. The earth is tilted at an angle of exactly 24 degrees, giving us the four seasons promised in Genesis 8:22. If the moon did not maintain its distance from the earth, the ocean tides would flood the earth twice a day. The surface of the earth is 70 percent water and 30 percent land. If the amount of water was significantly more, the earth would be a swamp. If it was significantly less, the earth would be a desert. Surely God is the master designer.

Suppose the law of gravity was so unreliable that we couldn't predict whether a falling object would go up or down. What if the law of biology that each brings forth after its own kind (stated 12 times in Genesis one) couldn't be depended upon, and the offspring of dogs might be dogs one time and monkeys the next? Or suppose we couldn't predict what kind of fruit a tree would produce from year to year.

God's Word is settled in heaven and on earth. Nature operates by fixed laws which God has established. These laws are as reliable as His Word. Just as the laws of nature remain unchanged for all generations, so God's Word is fixed forever. All of man's efforts can no more alter God's Word than they can alter the law of gravity.

Thy Word once spoken still stands
Unchanged from age to age,
Inscribed by man's faithful hands,
Delivered to us on sacred page.

C. Its Faithfulness is Proven v.91

They continue this day according to Your ordinances, for all are Your servants. The "they" referred to in this verse are heaven, mentioned in verse 89, and earth, mentioned in verse 90. God not only created and established the heavens and the earth, but He sustains them so that they operate with precision and power. Since He established the laws of nature, God can suspend or supersede them at His pleasure, as He did when the sun stood still in the time of Joshua, and when Jesus spoke to the winds and calmed the sea.

We see the proof of God's faithful word every time we see a sunrise or sunset or feel the wind or the rain on our faces. "Thus says the Lord who gives the light by day, the ordinances of the moon and the stars for a light by night, who disturbs the sea and its waves roar. The Lord of hosts is His name. If those ordinances depart from me says the Lord, then the seed of Israel shall also cease" (Jer.31:35-36).

Heaven and earth are God's servants and all things in them obey Him except man. The sun and the moon keep His laws, and the winds and the sea obey Him. Only man rebels and refuses to obey.

Spurgeon said, "By that word which is settled in heaven, may we be settled; by that voice which established the earth, may we be established, and by that command which all created beings obey, may we be made the servants of the Lord God Almighty."

The earth was created and fashioned by His power. It is now sustained by the word of His promise. And His promises are as reliable as His power.

All heaven and earth obeys
Every word Thou hast spoken.
Thy creation never strays,
And Thy law is never broken.

II. THE REVIEW OF GOD'S FAITHFUL WORD VS.92-93

A. It Brought the Psalmist Rejoicing v.92

Unless Your law had been my delight I would have perished in my affliction. The Word of God which sustains the universe in verses 89-91, sustains the psalmist in his affliction. It's not just his knowledge of law, but his delight in it that preserved him. He found delight in the Word when all other delights were taken from him.

In our counsel to those in affliction we must limit our counsel to the Word of God. If we don't we may bring them false comfort. Our own wisdom is faulty, but God's Word is a never ending source of comfort and hope to those who delight in it.

Alexander Wallace (p.324-325 Spurgeon's Treasury of David) tells of visiting a town in Scotland when times were very hard. A few coins were handed out each day to the very poor. A widow had received her daily pittance and went to the store to buy her daily supply of food. When she had only a penny left she cheerfully said, "Now I must buy oil with this that I may see to read my Bible during these long dark nights, for it's my only comfort now that every other comfort is gone away."

So it was with the psalmist.

> Affliction has been my plight
> And I feared that I would perish.
> Now Thy law is my delight
> And Thy words I greatly cherish.

B. It Brought the Psalmist Revival v.93

I will never forget Your precepts, for by them You have given me life. In the previous verse, the psalmist declared his delight in the Word. In this one he says he will never forget it. We never forget the things that bring us delight. We may study God's Word and even teach it and yet forget it if we don't delight in it. However, if we delight in it, it will renew our lives from day to day and we'll never forget it. Note that it wasn't the precepts that actually renewed the psalmist's life. They were only the instruments of life. God is the life-giving power. The precepts are the channel through which God life comes.

God's Word which activates and sustains the universe sustained the psalmist. The Word never changes, but it changes us and the world around us. It is, "quick and powerful and sharper than a two-edged sword" (Heb.4:12). Jesus said, "The words that I speak to you are spirit and they are life" (John 6:64). Jesus spoke words of life to the dead. To

Lazarus at the tomb he said, "Lazarus, come forth," and he came out of the tomb. To Jairus' daughter he said, "Maid, arise," and she arose.

His words which delivered these from the chains of death can also break the grip of sin and spiritual death for those who hear them and believe.

> Thy precepts I'll never forget,
> For it's by them that I live.
> I'll obey them without regret,
> And to Thee all glory give.

III. THE RESPONSE TO GOD'S FAITHFUL WORD VS. 94-96

A. The Psalmist Pursued God's Word v.94

I am Yours, save me, for I have sought Your precepts. The psalmist's plea for deliverance isn't based on his own goodness, but on his relationship to God. Notice that he doesn't say, "You are mine," but "I am Yours." He asks God to save that which is His own. Since he is God's possession, he is confident that the Lord will save him.

David repeatedly cried out for God to deliver him. "This poor man cried out and the Lord heard him and saved him out of all his troubles" (Ps. 34:6). And, "As for me, I will call upon God, and the Lord shall save me. Evening and morning and at noon I will pray and cry aloud" (Ps.55:16-17).

"Save me!" It's a short prayer – two words in English and only one in Hebrew. Real prayer doesn't consist of making speeches to God. The thief on the cross simply said, "Lord, remember me when You come into Your kingdom" (Luke 23:42).The desperate Canaanite woman who asked Jesus to heal her daughter in Matthew 15, cried out, "Lord, help me!" The Lord hears our cries no matter how short or how feeble they may be.

> Hear me Lord, for I am Thine,
> And deliver me now I pray.
> Thy precepts line upon line,
> I have sought every day.

B. The Psalmist Perused God's Word v. 95

The wicked wait for me to destroy me, but I will consider Your testimonies. The wicked had a plan to destroy the psalmist and they were waiting for an opportunity to use it. They were like robbers waiting beside the road for him. Evil men, like the devil, are patient and persistent. If they fail once they will come back again and again. Peter said, "Be sober, be vigilant, because your adversary, the devil, is like a roaring lion seeking whom he may devour" (I Peter 5:8).

God's testimonies are the psalmist's defense. If Satan can divert us from the Word he can destroy us. The psalmist is determined to focus on God's Word in all circumstances. He won't allow his attention to be diverted by danger. Nothing will keep him from God's precepts.

In verse 84, he spoke of seeking the Lord's precepts. In this verse, he speaks of considering them. The word "consider" comes from the Hebrew word *biyn* which means to inquire into, to consider diligently or to discern the deeper aspects of something. It's a step beyond the seeking of the previous verse. It's very close to our word "peruse" which I have used in the heading for this verse. The idea is to scrutinize or examine carefully. Many read the Bible and discuss it, but very few scrutinize it. That's what the psalmist was doing here, and he found comfort and protection in doing it.

> The wicked plot against me,
> And my life they seek to destroy,
> But I put my trust in Thee,
> And by Thy Word escape their ploy.

C. The Psalmist Proclaimed God's Word v.96

I have seen the consummation of all perfection, but Your commandment is exceedingly broad. The word "consummation" is from the Hebrew word *qus* which means to limit or put a boundary around something. The Hebrew word for "perfection" is *tichlah*. It's used in this form only here in the Old Testament, although other forms are used elsewhere. It means completion. There's a limit to every earthly enterprise. All man's theories, ideologies, philosophies, religions and achievements will run their course and come to an end. There's no lasting value in any of them.

This is also true in a moral sense. Man's goodness is limited and inadequate. Men think they are good only because they measure themselves with their own ruler, and weigh their goodness on a false scale. When measured by God's perfect law we all fall short.

While everything concerning man is limited and narrow, God's commandment is exceedingly broad. In verses 89-91, the psalmist speaks of the length of God's Word. Here he speaks of its width. It's not only eternal in length, it's infinitely wide. After scrutinizing it in verse 95, he concludes that there is far more to God's Word that first meets the eye. In this verse he contrasts man's idea of perfection with the real perfection found in God's commandments. He proclaims that God's Word is superior to all the world has to offer. It's broad enough to meet every need. It touches every word, action, thought and feeling that man may experience.

God's Word is faithful in every circumstance of life, and it always will be. The psalmist clings to it as his only source of comfort and hope.

On earth there is no perfection.
All that man does must end.
So it goes without any question,
That on God's Word I depend.

STANZA 13: PSALM 119: 97-104

THE WAY OF A WISE MAN

I. The Wise Man's Wisdom vs.97-100
  A. The Source of His Wisdom v.97
  B. The Superiority of His Wisdom vs.98-100
    1. Superior to his persecutors v.98
    2. Superior to his professors v.99
    3. Superior to his predecessors v.100
II. The Wise Man's Walk vs.101-104
  A. His Wise Actions vs.101-102
    1. What he avoided v.101
    2. What he approved v.102
  B. His Wise Affections vs.103-104
    1. What pleased him v.103
    2. What pained him v.104

There is no prayer or complaint in this stanza. It's full of joy and love for the law. The psalmist has moved from the valley to the mountain top. He has run the gauntlet of trials, persecution and unnamed afflictions, and has found comfort in God's Word. In verse 96, he gets a new revelation of the perfection and completeness of God's law. Now he declares his love for the law that has made him wise.

I. THE WISE MAN'S WISDOM VS.97-100

A. The Source of His Wisdom v.97

O how I love Your law! It is my meditation all the day. The psalmist bursts out in an exclamation expressing his intense love for God's law. His emotions are inexpressible. The word "how" denotes a measure that can't be expressed. It's like the "God so loved" in John 3:16. "How much" and "so much" are beyond measure. He loves the law because of its wisdom. His afflictions have driven him to the Word, and the Word has made him wise.

However, his wisdom didn't come from just reading the Word. It came from loving it and meditating on it. The more he meditated on it the more he loved it, and the more he loved it the more he meditated on it. His morning devotions, his noonday thoughts and his evening prayers were filled with it. Even his daily activities were saturated with it.

The combination of love for the Word and meditation on it give birth to wisdom. We won't become wise by just reading a few verses each morning to pump us up for the day. When the Bible isn't in our hands it must be in our minds and our hearts. Only then will we grow wise.

O how I love Thy law,
It's my meditation all day.
It alone is without flaw,
And reveals to me Thy way.

B. The Superiority of His Wisdom vs.98-100
  1. Superior to that of his persecutors v.98
You, through Your commandments, make me wiser than my enemies for they are ever with me. God made the psalmist wise, and His commandments were the channels of His wisdom. The commandments were the textbook, but God was his teacher. Studying can give us knowledge, but only God can make us wise. "Behold, the fear of the Lord, that is wisdom, and to depart from evil is understanding" (Job 28:28). "The fear of the Lord is the beginning of wisdom, a good understanding have all who do His commandments" (Ps. 111:10). "For the Lord gives wisdom. From His mouth comes knowledge and understanding" (Prov.2:6). It's clear from these verses that wisdom comes from God. But it doesn't come from just knowing God's commandments. It comes from keeping them.

In the Old Testament wisdom was the practical application of knowledge. The commandments weren't just declarations, they were practical principles for daily living. It's illustrated in the early life of David when it was said of him that "he behaved wisely in all his ways" (I Sam. 18:5,14).

Moses instructed Israel in the ways of wisdom. "Surely I have taught you statutes and judgments, just as the Lord commanded me that you should act according to them in the land which you go in to possess. Therefore, be careful to observe them; for this is your wisdom and your understanding in the sight of the peoples who will hear all these statutes and say, 'Surely this great nation is a wise and understanding people'" (Deut. 4:5-6).

The psalmist's enemies slandered him and set traps for him. He couldn't match them in deceitfulness. They learned deception in the school of lies. He had gone to another school, and learned from another teacher, that God's truth will always defeat scheming and deceit. Obedience to God's commandments is a better defense than retaliation.

Since he meditated on the commandments all day they were always in his mind and heart. As a soldier in battle must never lay aside his armor and weapons, so the Christian must make God's Word his constant companion.

Jesus was the embodiment of divine wisdom. The Word was in His heart to overcome temptation and spring the traps of the Pharisees without getting caught by their schemes.

> Thou hast made me wise,
> By obedience to Thy Word.
> The plots they devise
> Have never yet occurred.

2. Superior to his professors v.99

I have more understanding than all my teachers for Your testimonies are my meditation. The psalmist isn't boasting; he's only saying that the understanding he has received from God's Word is superior to what he has received from his teachers. He doesn't say he has more knowledge than his teachers, only that he has more understanding. True teachers are honored when their students excel them in wisdom. It's a mark of their success.

God's wisdom is greater wisdom than any human teacher can give. Many great teachers have knowledge, but lack understanding of how to apply it. I once knew a man who taught computer science in a university, yet had no idea about how to use a computer. His knowledge was only theoretical. There are even Bible teachers who can explain the Bible clearly without it having any impact on their lives.

The psalmist again stresses that meditation is the channel through God's wisdom flows into his heart. We may sit under great teachers and still remain fools if we don't meditate on the words we read and hear.

The wisdom from God's Word
Is not what any man may teach,
For his ears have not heard,
Nor his tongue uttered such speech.

3. Superior to his predecessors v.100

I understand more than the ancients because I keep your precepts. The Hebrew word translated "ancients" here refers to old men, not to men of ancient times. Old is not synonymous with wise, although we sometimes speak as if though they were the same. We are familiar with the saying that "there's no fool like an old fool." The writer of Ecclesiastes said, "Better a poor and wise youth than an old and foolish king who will be admonished no more" (Eccl. 4:13).

The psalmist was in no way discounting the old and wise. The old have studied much, experienced much and observed much. However, the psalmist is saying the wisdom that comes from God, the ancient of days, is superior to that which comes from ancient men whose days are like the mist of the morning that appears for a little while and is gone.

Job said, "I said, 'age should speak, and multitude of years should teach wisdom, but there is a spirit in man, and the breath of the Almighty gives him understanding. Great men are not always wise, nor do the aged always understand justice'" (Job 32:7-9).

Solomon received great wisdom at age 20, but he was an old fool at 60 because his many wives turned his heart away from the Lord to false gods. At age 12, Jesus sat in the Temple with the old and wise, listening and asking questions. "And all that heard Him were astonished at His understanding and answers" (Luke 2:47).

Zeneck says, "True wisdom does not depend on a lifelong experience, but rather upon obedience to God's precepts." Most of us who are older can identify with the saying, "Too soon old and too late wise." Unfortunately, many who have known the Lord for 50 to 60 years, or longer, have not grown wise in the things of God. They don't open their hearts to greater wisdom. They walk in the same paths and repeat the same mistakes year after year.

The psalmist again states that his understanding comes from keeping God's precepts. The young who obey God's Word become wiser than the old who only study it.

Thou hast made me wise
Above those who are old,
For it's Thy Word I prize
More than silver and gold.

II. THE WISE MAN'S WALK VS. 101-104

A. His Wise Actions vs.101-102
 1. What he avoided v.101
I have restrained my feet from every evil way that I may keep Your word. The proof of our wisdom is in our walk, not our talk. The natural direction of our feet is toward evil, so they must be restrained. The word "restrained" is a strong word that's sometimes used to describe chains or fetters. The broad road is more attractive and our feet will wander on to it unless they are restrained. Note that this isn't a promise of what the psalmist intends to do, but a statement of what he has already done.

He has avoided every evil way. He knew he couldn't deviate from the law even in the smallest matter. Paul said, "Abhor what is evil" (Rom. 12:9). And, "Abstain from every form of evil" (I Thess. 5:22). The idea is not a slavish observance of rules as the Pharisees did, but rather the keeping of God's Word as He intended. Jesus violated many of the traditions of the Pharisees, but kept God's law perfectly.

The principle here is that if we want to keep God's Word we need to avoid actions that will lead us in the direction of disobedience. A man who lived high on a mountain needed to hire a driver for his coach. The road leading to his house was narrow, and sometimes ran along the edge of a cliff. He asked the first applicant how close he could drive to the edge of the cliff he could drive without going over. "I believe I could get as close as two feet," the man replied. He called in a second applicant and asked the same question. "I could come within a foot of the edge," he said. The man repeated the question to a third applicant. "If you want a driver who will drive close to that cliff you should get someone else," he answered. "I'll drive as far away from the edge as possible." The man hired him immediately.

Keeping God's Word requires discipline and restraint. There are dangers we have to avoid if we are to walk on the narrow road of obedience.

O Lord, I have turned my feet
From every evil way,
That I may not know defeat,
Or Thy Word disobey.

2. What he approved v.102

I have not departed from Your judgments, for You yourself have taught me. This is the other side of verse 101. First, "I have restrained." Now, "I have not departed." The holy walk is both positive and negative. When we refrain from taking the first step toward evil we are drawn closer to God's Word.

We don't live without sin, but if we are true believers we won't forsake God's ways and live a life of disobedience. God's Word is adequate for all our needs so there's no need to seek satisfaction in the world. "Therefore, you shall be careful to do as the Lord has commanded you. You shall not turn aside to the right hand or to the left" (Deut. 5:32).

The psalmist has previously asked the Lord to teach him (vs.26,33,64,68). Now he declares that He has done so. He says, "You Yourself have taught me." The Lord didn't send him an instructional video and do-it-yourself manual. He was his personal teacher. Every believer has a personal teacher in the person of the Holy Spirit. Jesus said, "But the Helper, the Holy Spirit, whom the Father will send in My name will teach you all things and bring to your remembrance all things that I said to you" (John 14:26).

The Lord taught the psalmist through affliction and by giving him insight into the Word. The two work together for his learning. When the Lord teaches us we are well taught and do not forget His lessons. However, we have not learned if we don't walk in His Word. "Teach me Your way O Lord; I will walk in Your truth. Unite my heart to fear Your name" (Ps.86:11).

God has gifted human teachers to teach His truth, but only He can illuminate our minds to receive it and walk in it. Paul said, "These things we also speak, not in words which man's wisdom teaches, but which the Holy Spirit speaks, comparing spiritual things with spiritual" (I Cor. 2:13).

Thy Word I've not forsaken,
For by Thee I've been taught.
By evil I've not been taken,
Nor in it's snares been caught.

B. His Wise Affections vs.103-104
 1. What pleased him v.103
How sweet are Your words to my taste, sweeter than honey to my mouth. The Hebrew word translated "sweet" here is *malas* which means smooth, pleasant, satisfying or delightful. It's used only here in the Old Testament. God's words were pleasant to the psalmist. They were satisfying to his soul. He has difficulty expressing his delight in it, so he says, "How sweet." It's not a question asked, but a superlative expressed.

The pleasantness of earthly knowledge is distasteful compared to the knowledge of God. However, sometimes we may cultivate the appetites of the flesh. We may feed our souls on the world's garbage and never cultivate a taste for the God's Word.

Ezekiel found God's Word to be sweet when he ate it. "Moreover, He said to me, 'Son of man, eat what you find; eat this scroll, and go, speak to the house of Israel.' So I opened my mouth and He caused me to eat that scroll ...so I ate, and in my mouth it was like honey in sweetness" (Ezek. 3:1-3). Of course, Ezekiel used eating the scroll as a metaphor for his devouring what was written on it. He found God's Word more desirable than the most delicious food.

Jeremiah had a similar experience. "Your words were found and I did eat them, and Your word was to me the joy and rejoicing of my heart" (Jer. 15:16). In Revelation 10, the angel gave John a little book and told him to eat it. "And I took the book out of the angel's hand and ate it, and it was as sweet as honey to my mouth. But when I had eaten it my stomach became bitter" (Rev. 10:10). Sometimes God's Word is sweet to the taste, but when we digest what it says, it has a bitter message.

The sweetness of honey isn't discovered by touch or smell, only by taste. So we don't discover the delights of God's Word by just hearing it. We must internalize it and digest it.

Thy words I once did eat,
And their taste was like honey.
Now they're my daily meat,
Which I buy without money.

2. What pained him v.104

Through Your precepts I get understanding, therefore, I hate every false way. This stanza begins with "I love Your law," and ends with "I hate every false way." The psalmist abhors every falsehood because God's precepts gave him an understanding of the truth.

The test of true wisdom is the ability to distinguish between the true and the false. That's what God's Word does. To love God and His Word is to hate falsehood. "You who love the Lord hate evil" (Ps.97:10).

Proverbs 7:7 describes the young man who lives an immoral life as "void of understanding."

Any lifestyle that doesn't conform to God's Word is a false way. False ways create false hopes of happiness. False ways are deceptive ways. They may seem right to the natural man, but they lead to disaster. "There is a way that seems right to a man, but its end is the way of death" (Prov. 14:12).

The more we understand God's Word, the more we will hate EVERY false way, not just some. We can't spit out some false ways and swallow others. We can't reject the false ways of others and accept our own. We can't give the devil any slack. We must reject all false opinions and practices. If we love God's law we will reject the ways of self-will, self-righteousness, self-seeking, worldliness and lust wherever we find them.

> Upon Thy Word I stand,
> And each day for thee I wait.
> I obey every command,
> For every false way I hate.

A LIGHT FOR DARK PLACES

I. The Light Reveals vs.105-106
  A. It Reveals Direction v.105
  B. It Requires Dedication v.106
II. The Light Revives vs.107-108
  A. The Pressure v.107a
  B. The Prayer v.107b
  C. The Praise v.108
III. The Light Rescues vs. 109 -110
  A. From Death v.109
  B. From Danger v.110
IV. The Light Rejoices vs. 111-112
  A. It's a Precious Possession v.111
  B. It's a Permanent Possession v.112

For the last two stanzas there has been a pause in the psalmist's afflictions and the assaults of his enemies. But in this stanza he descends again into a dark and dangerous world. He must walk through the night, but God's Word lights his way.

I. THE LIGHT REVEALS VS.105-106

A. It Reveals Direction v.105

Your word is a lamp to my feet and a light to my path. First, the Word is a lamp. In Bible times a lamp was a small bowl containing oil and a wick. It provided a limited amount of light over a small area. It focused light on the next step of a dark path. In more recent times travelers carried torches or lanterns to avoid falling into ditches or stumbling over things in the road. Now, of course, we have lighted streets and roads. God's Word guides us step by step through the darkness and helps us avoid the snares of the evil one. Solomon said, "For the commandment is a lamp, and the law a light" (Prove. 6:23).

Second, the Word is a light. The word" light" used here denotes a more diffused light than a lamp provides. It's like a full moon that chases away the dark shadows along the road ahead. It keeps the traveler from wandering off course. God's Word is a light to give us the direction we need, and a lamp to show us the things we must avoid along the way. It's a heavenly light shining in a dark world.

There's no substitute for the light of God's Word. In verse 130, the psalmist says, "The entrance of Your word gives light; it gives understanding to the simple." Others may turn on the light for us, but we must walk in it. The lamp must be kept burning and bright by constant study and meditation. A lamp doesn't shine on the path if it remains on the shelf.

Spurgeon said, "The head needs illumination, but even more, the feet need direction, else head and feet may both fall into a ditch." Knowledge of the Word without obedience, won't keep us safe in this dark and dangerous world

> Thy Word gives me light
> And illuminates my way.
> It reveals the right,
> No matter what others say.

B. It Requires Dedication v.106

I have sworn and confirmed that I will keep Your righteous judgments. It's easy to see the light, but it requires a high degree of dedication to walk in it. The psalmist has taken a solemn oath that he will walk in the light. He will follow only the path upon which the light of God's Word is shining.

The Scriptures are a record of God's righteous judgments. They report His declarations and dealings with men. They are His verdicts on questions of good and evil, and they are always right. The psalmist resolved to follow them at any cost. To know God's Word is to know God's will, and to keep it is to do God's will.

Most commentators view this as a vow of the psalmist to obey God's Word. It's more than a vow. It's an oath. Oaths are used in different ways in the Scriptures as well as today. In a court of law we swear to tell the truth. When we take an oath of office we swear to perform the duties of that office. An oath of office usually states the duties of the office and ends by saying, "so help me God." This seems to be the sense here. The psalmist is declaring that with God's help he will keep His judgments. It's only with God's help that any of us can obey His Word. Our ability to fulfill our intentions ultimately lies in God's faithfulness.

With a heart now twice born,
Filled with holy desires,
To keep Thy Word I've sworn,
And do all it requires.

II. THE LIGHT REVIVES VS.107-108

A. The Pressure v.107a

I am afflicted very much. As soon as he swears obedience to God's Word the psalmist is called on to suffer great affliction. The more he resolves to obey, the greater his affliction seems to be. He doesn't mention the nature of his affliction, but in the past it's mostly been in the form of suffering inflicted at the hands of his enemies. That would seem to fit here since the more determined we are to serve the Lord, the more our enemies resist our efforts.

Stones don't fit into buildings unless they are chiseled. Gold must be refined by fire before it's pure, and vines pruned before they can bear good fruit. Paul said, "But we glory also in tribulation, knowing that tribulation produces perseverance, and perseverance character, and character hope" (Rom. 5:3-4). The

17th Century Scottish preacher and scholar, Robert Leighton, said, "Affliction is the diamond dust that heaven polishes its jewels with."

B. The Prayer v.107b

Revive me, O Lord, according to Your word. It's a prayer he has prayed several times before (vs.57,40,88). In his great affliction he needs a new infusion of life and strength to endure. He calls upon the Lord to act according to the promises and principles of His Word. Indeed, the Word itself will strengthen and revive us in our afflictions.

Lord, my affliction is great.
Restore my strength I pray,
For it's upon Thee I wait,
And trust Thee day by day.

C. The Praise v.108

Accept, I pray the freewill offerings of my mouth, and teach me Your judgments. The word "accept" means to be pleased with or take pleasure in. The psalmist knew that there was more to worship than the offerings of sheep or oxen as burnt offerings. When the people's hearts were not right with God, their burnt offerings were rejected. He believed the true condition of the heart was better expressed through the sacrifices of the mouth. The writer of Hebrews agrees. "Therefore, by Him let us continually offer the sacrifice of praise to God, that is, the fruit of our lips, giving thanks to His name" (Heb.13:15).

Praise to God must be given freely, without compulsion or constraint. There is no acceptance without willingness. Spurgeon said, "God's revenues are not derived from forced taxation, but from free-will donation." The offerings of the lips don't depend on the circumstances of our lives. No temple or alter is needed. A jail cell will do just as well as Paul and Silas discovered (Acts 16:25). The psalmist lifted his verbal offerings to heaven in a time when he was suffering great affliction.

Praise without knowledge is incomplete worship, so the psalmist asked the Lord to teach him. Biblical knowledge and praise go together. Many of the great hymns have been replaced today with emotional music that repeats slogans and words without biblical content. We need to be taught until our songs reflect knowledge of God and our praises are more than empty words.

> O Lord, I lift my voice
> And offer to Thee my praise.
> I worship Thee by choice,
> So teach me all Thy ways.

III. THE LIGHT RESCUES VS.109-110

A. From Death v.109

My life is continually in my hand, yet I do not forget Your law. This is a proverbial saying meaning that his life is in constant danger. Anything held in the hand is in danger of being dropped or snatched away. The psalmist faced life-threatening dangers from his enemies. We too live in a dangerous world. Even greater than the physical dangers are the spiritual dangers that can destroy our relationship with God.

Yet the psalmist doesn't forget God's law. Even when his life is in danger, God's law is in his heart. In time of danger he keeps his resolve to obey it. Life threatening conditions don't exempt us from doing right even when sin offers safety. Our lives may be at risk in our own hands, but they are safe in God's hands. If we remember His Word when we face death, we can be sure He will remember us.

> Even when death I face,
> Thy law I will not forget.
> I will Thy Word embrace,
> For on it my heart is set.

B. From Danger v.110

The wicked have laid a snare for me, but I wandered not from Your precepts. The psalmist's life is in danger because the wicked are setting traps for him. If his enemies can't destroy him by violence, they will resort to cunning and deceit. Saul set traps for David. Daniel's political enemies set a trap for him. The Pharisees set traps for Jesus, and the Jews set them for Paul.

Traps are the tools of the devil, and life is full of them. There are basically two kinds of traps. The first are set where we walk. They are the nooses that catch our feet, and the pits dug in our paths and hidden from our view. These are the traps that grow out of our daily circumstances and relationships.

The second are set in what we want. They offer bait to lure us to the unseen hook or trap. The bait appeals to the lust of the eyes, the lust of the flesh or the pride of life. (See I John 2:16).

Trapping animals is not acceptable today, but it was 60 years ago. As a kid I trapped small animals – opossums, skunks and mink – for their fur. I set the traps and carefully covered them with leaves or grass. Nearby, I placed the bait to lure them to the place where the trap was set.

If we don't take the enemy's bait we won't be snared by his traps. Paul warned the Corinthians not to be ignorant of the devil's devices (II Cor. 2:1). He also told them no temptation was so strong that they would not be able to bear it (I Cor. 10:13).

When we wander from God's precepts we fall into the devil's traps. God puts no snares in our paths. His precepts shine on our pathways and reveal the traps of the enemy. The psalmist had already declared that he had hidden God's Word in his heart that he might not sin (v.11). If we wander from God's precepts we remove ourselves from the His light shinning on our paths.

> Many snares surround me,
> But from Thy Word I do not stray,
> And by its light I can see
> Every pitfall along the way.

IV. THE LIGHT REJOICES VS, 111-112

A. It's A Precious Possession v.111

Your testimonies I have taken as a heritage forever, for they are the rejoicing of my heart. This verse is related to verse 57 where the psalmist speaks of God as his portion. However, there is a different emphasis here. The Promised Land was divided by lot and each tribe and family received a portion as its inheritance to be passed from generation to generation. Although each tribe was given its portion as an inheritance, it still had to take it from the Canaanites.

He is saying that he is taking God's testimonies as his heritage which is an even greater heritage than the land. The Word of God was an inheritance he had chosen and it could never be taken away. It was his most precious possession. The same inheritance is available to each of us, but we must choose to take it. Many of us are like Esau, who considered God's inheritance of such little value that he traded it for a bowl of stew.

A man died and gave his old Bible to his son as his inheritance. Disappointed, the son put the Bible in an old trunk. Years later, he fell upon hard times and decided to read his father's Bible in search of an answer. He dug it out of the trunk and opened it and began to read. Between its pages he found thousands of dollars in $100 bills. God's Word is a valuable inheritance, but only if we study it and claim its promises.

It's an everlasting treasure – an eternal inheritance that can never be taken away. Peter spoke of the Word of God which lives and abides forever (I Peter 1:23). Jesus said, "Heaven and earth shall pass away, but My words shall by no means pass away" Matt. 24:35).

We can know what kind of a person one is by what he or she enjoys the most. A man or woman who finds joy in God's testimonies, which can never be taken away, will always have joy no matter what happens. Paul could write his joy-filled letter to the Philippians from a Roman jail cell and say, "Rejoice in the Lord always. Again, I say rejoice" (Phil. 4:4).

> Lord, Thy Word is my treasure.
> I have made it my choice.
> Its value has no measure,
> In it I'll always rejoice.

B. It's A Permanent Possession v.112

I have inclined my heart to perform Your statutes forever, to the very end. In verse 36, the psalmist asks God to incline his heart. Here he says that HE has inclined it. Both are true. We can't incline what God has not inclined. He has resolved to follow the inclination God has given him rather than the sinful inclinations of his own heart. God gives us a new heart, but we must keep it diligently (Prov. 4:23). The field won't produce fruit without hard work by the farmer. So we, by prayer, study, and meditation, must incline our own hearts to produce fruit. As with the heritage of verse 111, God gives it, but we must possess it.

We can't do what our hearts are not inclined to do. "Therefore, my beloved brethren, you have always obeyed, not in my presence only, but how much more in my absence. Work out your own salvation with fear and trembling, for it is God who works in you both to will and to do His good pleasure" (Phil.2:12-13).

The psalmist has purposed to obey God's statutes to the very end. He has vowed to obey, not just by performing heroic deeds, but in the daily plodding and drudgery of life. He could say with Paul, "I have fought a good fight, I have finished the course, I have kept the faith" (II Tim. 4:7). His resolve isn't a promise made when he's in a jam, or during an emotional high. It's a holy resolve to walk in the light of God's Word until the end. It's a lifetime commitment, not just something he wanted to try for a while.

Spurgeon said, "Many are inclined to preach, but the psalmist was inclined to practice; many are inclined to perform ceremonies, but he is inclined to perform statutes; many are inclined to obey occasionally, but he is inclined to obey, and to obey always."

To keep Thy statutes always
In my heart I have resolved,
To the end of all my days,
Or until time is dissolved.

STANZA 15: PSALM 119:113-120

HELP IN TIME OF DANGER

Introduction v.113
    1. What the psalmist's loathed v.113a
    2. What the psalmist's loved v.113b
I. God Shields the Psalmist vs. 114-115
  A. The Shield Explained v.114
    1. The Lord's person was his sanctuary v.114a
    2. The Lord's presence was his shield v.114b
    3. The Lord's promise was his security v.114c
  B. The Shield Experienced v.115
    1. His fearless speech v.115a
    2. His faithful service v.115b
II. God Supports the Psalmist vs.116-117
  A. By Giving Him Strength v.116
  B. By Giving Him Safety v.117
III. God Separates the Psalmist vs. 118-119

A. From the Wandering v.118
B. From the Wicked v. 119
Conclusion v.120 The Psalmist's Fear

INTRODUCTION V.113

The structure of this stanza is complex, but its contents are rich, and its study rewarding. Zemek says it's like the currents and eddies of a great river with its headwaters in verse 113, quickly branching out into two tributaries. It's a study in contrasts between what the psalmist loved and what he hated.

1. What the psalmist loathed v.113a
I hate the double-minded. In verses 104 and 128, the psalmist says he hates every false way. In verse 168, he says he hates lying. False ways and lying are set in contrast to God's Word. Here he says he hates the double-minded. He uses the same Hebrew word Elijah used on Mount Carmel when he asked the people how long they would halt between two opinions. It describes those who will sail in the direction of any wind. They both run with the rabbit and hunt with the hounds. They are in a constant state of wavering. James says, "The double-minded man is unstable in all his ways" (James 1:8).

2. What the psalmist loves v.113b
But I love Your law. God's law stands in sharp contrast to the wavering ways of men. He who hates

the unstable ways of evil men will love God's law. It's the infallible measure for right and wrong. In science, today's truth was yesterday's error. In the ethical systems of men, right and wrong are relative, but God's truth is unchanging. Love for God's law gives us stability and serves as an anchor for our lives.

It is God's law I love,
For it alone is right.
It's given from above,
And to earth it brings light.

I. GOD SHIELDS THE PSALMIST
VS.114-115

A. The Shield Explained v.114
 1. The Lord's person was his sanctuary v.114a
You are my hiding place. This suggests a place away from the battle where the enemy can't intrude – a place where he can be alone with God. The Hebrew word for hiding place is *seter* which means a covering or a secret hiding place. It most frequently pictures God as a place of refuge and protection from all danger. It's a place we all need to discover, not only for refuge, but for refreshment.

The prophet Isaiah spoke of such a place for God's people. "Come my people, enter your chambers, and shut your doors behind you. Hide yourselves, as it were, for a little moment until the indignation is past" (Isa. 26:20). David also spoke of a sanctuary of the soul when he said, "You are my hiding place. You shall preserve me from trouble.You shall surround me with songs of deliverance" (Ps.32:7). And again, "For in the time of trouble He shall hide me in His pavilion; in the secret place of His tabernacle He shall hide me" (Ps. 27:5).

2. The Lord's presence was his shield v.114b

And my shield. The Hebrew word for shield is *magen,* which means a surrounding. The psalmist could not always be hidden away. There were battles to fight, and when in battle the Lord was his shield. David said in Psalm 5:12, "For You O Lord, will bless the righteous with favor; with favor You will surround him as a shield." God told Abraham that He would be his "shield and his reward" (Gen.15:1).

God has been a shield for His people in every generation. He said, "Because you have made the Lord, who is my refuge, even the Most High, your dwelling place, No evil shall befall you, nor shall any plague come near your dwelling; for He gives His angels charge over you to keep you in all your ways" (Ps.91:9-10).

God's angels shield us from harm. In II Kings 6, the Syrian Army surrounded the city where Elisha was. When his servant saw the city was surrounded, he cried out, "Alas, my master, what shall we do?" Elisha replied, "Do not fear. Those who are with us are more than those who are with them." He then prayed that the Lord would open the young man's eyes. When his eyes were opened he saw the mountain filled with the horses and chariots of the Lord.

God sent an angel to muzzle the lions in the den where Daniel spent the night, and to shield Shadrach, Meshach and Abed-Nego from the flames of the furnace. God sent His angel into Peter's prison cell to free him the night before he was scheduled to be killed.

God continues to shield his faithful servants today. In his book, "God's Smuggler," Brother Andrew tells how the Lord blinded the border guards as he and his companions smuggled Bibles into communist countries. In his book, "Arthur the Pilgrim," Arthur Blessitt tells how others saw angels standing guard around him at night as he carried the cross through war ravaged countries preaching, and distributing Bibles and tracts.

It's still as Isaiah promised, "In righteousness you shall be established. You shall be far from oppression, for you shall not fear, and from terror for it shall not come near you....No weapon formed against you shall prosper, and every tongue which rises against you in judgment you shall condemn. This is the heritage of the servants of the Lord" (Isa. 54:14,17).

3. The Lord's promise was his security v.114c

I hope in Your word. The word hope, as it's used today, means little more than a fleeting wish. We may say, "I hope it rains today," which is another way of saying, "I wish it would rain today." But hope, as it's used in the Bible, conveys the idea of certainty based on God's promises. When the psalmist says, "I hope in Your word," he's certain that God will be his shelter and his shield in the future just as He has been in the past. The reason for his certainty is that God's Word has promised it. It's a provision of God's covenant, so it's his heritage.

As we face dangers and difficulties in life, we too can hope in God's Word, knowing He will keep His promises.

In the secret place
I find shelter and a shield.
There I see His face,
As His presence is revealed.

B. The Shield Experienced v.115
 1. His fearless speech v.115a
Depart from me you evildoers. The psalmist has been addressing God. Now, embolden by his assurance that God is his shelter and shield, he speaks to the evildoers. The root meaning of the word for evildoers is to be broken and useless, good for nothing like a broken tree limb.

The psalmist will not keep company with them and boldly tells them to depart. Paul said, "What fellowship has righteousness with lawlessness? And what communion has light with darkness? Or what part has a believer with an unbeliever?..Come out from among them and be separate" (II Cor.6:14-17).

If we boldly take our stand against evil we may be ridiculed. However, we won't be half as miserable as the believer who tries to please both God and the world. Christians who walk in the counsel of the ungodly, stand in the way of sinners or sit in the seat of the scornful, (Ps.1:1) are as miserable as a fox in a dog kennel. Sometimes, when we take a bold stand for Christ, the wicked will flee from us like bugs flee the light. At other times we must tell them to go away.

2. His faithful service v.115b

For I will keep the commandments of my God. Free from the influence of evildoers, and armed with the assurance that God will protect him, the psalmist feels a greater freedom to obey God's commandments. When we separate ourselves from evil and take God at His word we are empowered with great boldness.

David Livingston, the famous missionary and explorer, plunged fearlessly into the heart of Africa because He believed the promise of Jesus to be with us unto the end of the world. He said he believed the promise because it was "the word of a perfect gentlemen."

This is the only place the expression "my God," is found in Psalm 119. It suggests a very personal relationship. When we make a wholehearted commitment to separate ourselves from evil and fully obey God's Word, we enter a new level in our relationship with our heavenly Father.

My God! How charming the sound.
How pleasant to repeat!
May the heart with pleasure bound,
Where God has fixed His seat.
–Quoted by Charles Spurgeon

II. GOD SUPPORTS THE PSALMIST
VS.116-117

A. By Giving Him strength v.116

Uphold me according to Your word that I may live, and do not let me be ashamed of my hope. In verse 115, he removed the external hindrances to obedience, now the psalmist asks for internal strength. "Uphold" means to sustain or bear up. Psalm 37:17 says, "The arms of the wicked will be broken, but the Lord upholds the righteous." And in verse 24 of the same psalm, "Though he fall he shall not utterly be cast down, for the Lord upholds him with His right hand." The idea is that the psalmist wants God to strengthen him and undergird him so he won't fall of his trials and temptations.

He asks, as he often does, for God to sustain his life according to His Word. He could mean according to the promises of His Word, the principles of His Word, or according to the examples given in His Word. If God has given us life, will He not also sustain it?

The psalmist's fear of shame comes back to haunt him again. His hope is in the promises of his God. Because of it, he has commanded the evildoers to leave him, and vowed to obey God's commandments. Now he fears that he will be ashamed because of his weakness and inability to fulfill his promise to obey.

We may have reasons to be ashamed – ashamed of our thoughts, our doubts, our words and our deeds – but we will never have reason to be ashamed of our hope, because it is based on the firm foundation of God's Word. In Psalm 25:1-2, David wrote, "Let me not be ashamed. Let not my enemies triumph over me. Indeed, let no one who waits on You be ashamed."

Of Thee I'm not ashamed.
Thy promises are sure.
With every trial named
Comes strength to endure.

B. By Giving Him Safety v.117

Hold me up and I shall be safe, and I shall observe Your statutes continually. First, the psalmist asks to be lifted up; now he asks to be held up. The word "hold up" is from a verb that means to sustain either by outward strength or inward refreshment. Sometimes we need one, and sometimes the other. God gives to us according to our needs.

We don't usually pray for safety unless we feel we are in danger. However, we may be in danger without realizing it. We live in a hostile world and are always subject to the temptations of the devil, the lure of the world and the lusts of the flesh. Our safety depends on God's holding us up, not our holding on to Him. It reminds us of Peter's attempt to walk on the water in Matthew 14:28-30. When he took his eyes off Christ and looked at the wind and the waves, he began to sink. Christ took him by the hand and lifted him up.

In Psalm 17:5, David wrote, "Uphold my steps in Your paths, that my footsteps may not slip." And, "By You I have been upheld from birth" (Psalm 71:6).

We find our greatest safety in obedience to God's Word. However, it's not found in occasional obedience, but continual obedience. The King James Version says, "I will have respect unto Thy statutes," meaning to look with favor on them. If we look with favor on them, we will keep them.

> In God I put my trust,
> And find safety every day.
> For all His ways are just,
> So His Word I will obey.

III. GOD SEPARATES THE PSALMIST
VS.118-119

A. From the Wandering v.118
You reject those who stray from Your statutes, for their deceit is falsehood. The King James uses the metaphor "trodden down" to describe their rejection of God's statutes. The righteous (who observe His statutes continually) are upheld, but those who stray from them are trodden down. It's a figure that describes what will eventually happen to all the enemies of God. They will be like Jezebel, thrown down and trodden under Jehu's chariot. They will become worthless like the chaff that is separated from the grain (Ps. 1:4), or like the salt that as lost its flavor and is good for nothing but to be thrown out and trampled underfoot by men (Matt.5:13).

To stray from the truth is to stray into falsehood. "Their deceit is falsehood" is a truism that states emphatically the delusional nature of lies. They are so deceived that they believe their own lies. They lie even when they gain nothing by it. Any deviation from God's statutes is a falsehood, no matter how many millions may believe otherwise. This is especially true in the last days when men will be given strong delusion and will believe lies.

You reject those who stray,
For they call Thy truth a lie.
Under Thy foot they lay,
And at Thy hand they will die.

B. From the Wicked v. 119

You will put away the wicked from the earth like dross; therefore, I love Your testimonies. In verse 115, the psalmist put the evildoers out of his own life, now he says that God will banish them from the earth. The same process that purifies the righteous destroys the wicked. As long as they are mixed with the righteous, the ungodly may be unnoticed, just as the dross is indistinguishable from unrefined gold. Only in the refining process is the true character of each revealed. The righteous come forth as pure gold, but the wicked are cast away as dross.

When God has finished His refining work, no dross will remain, and no saint will be impure. Wickedness will be put away from us, and the wicked will be put away from God. In Malachi 3:3, the Lord says, speaking of Christ, "He will sit as a refiner and a purifier of silver. He will purify the sons of Levi, and purge them as gold and silver." The day will come when the Lord will separate the gold from the dross.

Russian merchants once passed off base metal coins to some Swedish traders. When the traders discovered the deception they melted the coins and threw the deceivers into the molten metal and cast them into the dump. Such is the final end of all deceivers.

The psalmist foresaw that final day of separation of the gold from the dross. But while he waits for it, he will love and obey God's testimonies. They promise that God will make all things right. They give examples that foreshadow how God will deal with the wicked at the final judgment. Above all, they give him, and us, instructions for right living.

> Remove from us the dross
> That we must now endure.
> We count it not as loss,
> That makes our hearts impure.

CONCLUSION V.120

My flesh trembles at the fear of You, and I am afraid of your judgments. It's not that the psalmist fears that God will judge him, but he trembles when he thinks of God's judgment upon those who don't fear Him – the double-minded, the evildoers and the wicked whom He will put away like dross.

He knows God is a consuming fire that will devour the wicked. The word "trembles" is the same word used in Job 4:15 where Job said, "The hair of my body stood up." Today we would say, "My hair stood on end." It's an expression of horror. Any believer who seriously considers the sins of our time ought to tremble in anticipation of God's coming judgment.

Psalm 91:8 says, "Only with your eyes shall you look and see the reward of the wicked." In Psalm 73, Aspah speaks of how he envied the wicked until he saw their end, how they were brought to sudden desolation and were consumed with terror, and he was grieved for them. Paul said, "Knowing the terror of the Lord, we persuade men" (II Cor. 5:11). We will not be effective in persuading the lost to be saved until we understand their eternal destiny.

My flesh is made to tremble
By those who God offend,
Who before Thy throne assemble
To contemplate their end.

THE RIGHT CONCLUSION

I. The Psalmist's Perplexing Dilemma vs.121-122
    A. The Situation Described v.121
    B. The Solution Desired v.122
II. The Psalmist's Passionate Desire vs. 123-125
    A. The Intensity Revealed v.123
    B. The Instruction Requested v.124
    C. The Insight Required v.125
III. The Psalmist's Presumptuous Demand v.126
    A. His Daring v.126a
    B. His Discernment v.126b
IV. The Psalmist's Priceless Discovery vs.127-128
    A. God's Word is Precious v.127
    B. God's Word is Perfect v.128

The psalmist has done the right thing, but others have oppressed him. It's a situation most of us face at one time or another. In this stanza he continues to trust God's Word despite being treated unfairly.

Verses 121 and 122 are two of the three verses in Psalm 119 that do not mention the law or one of the synonyms for it.

I. THE PSALMIST'S PERPLEXING DILEMMA VS.121-122

A. The Situation Described v.121

I have done justice and righteousness; do not leave me to my oppressors. The KJV says, "I have done judgment and justice." The two Hebrew words *mispat* and *sedeq,* are used together 20 times in the Old Testament. *Mispat* refers to the law by which judgments are pronounced, and *sedeq* refers to the fairness with which the judgments are applied (See Deut.1:16).

Justice and righteousness are the foundation stones of God's rule. Psalm 89:14 says, "Righteousness and justice are the foundation of Your throne." According to II Samuel 8:15, they were the guiding principles of David's kingdom. "David reigned over all Israel and David administered judgment and justice to all his people."

Judgment and justice are more important than worship and sacrifice. "To do righteousness and justice is more acceptable unto the Lord than sacrifice" (Prov. 21:3). And, "Behold, a king will still reign in righteousness and princes will rule with justice" (Isa. 32:11). As you can see, justice and righteousness are words often used to describe how kings and other leaders should rule.

The psalmist had made just decisions and had carried them out fairly, but he is not being treated fairly by others. Instead, he is being oppressed and asks God not to abandon him to his oppressors. The word translated "oppressors" is *asaq,* which means those who extort, exploit or abuse. The next verse identifies them with the proud.

He has dealt with others fairly. Now he asks that he be delivered from those who treat him unfairly. If we treat others fairly we may sometimes be treated unfairly, but we can be certain that God will not abandon us to them.

Lord, to Thy Word I have been true,
And to others I have been fair.
Give to my oppressors their due
That I might not their abuses bear.

B. The Solution Desired v.122

Be surety for Your servant for good; Do not let the proud oppress me. The word for "surety" is *arab.* The root meaning is to weave together or entwine. It implies a relationship whereby one person's interests and resources are entwined with those of another as when one becomes the guarantor of a loan for another. Six times in Proverbs Solomon warned us not to enter into such relationships, especially in financial matters.

Job cried to God, "Put down a pledge for me with yourself" (Job 17:3). Hezekiah said, "My eyes fail from looking upward. O Lord, I am oppressed; Undertake for me" (Isa. 38:14).

The psalmist is so desperate that he believes his only hope is for the Lord to become his surety. He positions himself as a servant without power or authority of his own.

The proud never give up. They have held him in great derision (v.51), forged a lie against him (v.69), and dug a pit for him (v.85). Now they oppress him. His only hope is that God will take up his cause. His hope is well founded because God hates a proud look (Prov. 6:17). He resists the proud but gives grace to the humble (James 4:6). When we call upon God to act in harmony with His nature and in accord with His Word, we can be sure of an answer.

The proud oppress the humble because they think their superiority gives them the right to oppress others in order to achieve their self-centered purposes. But God is against them, and will bring them down in His own time. If we want God to take up our cause we must walk humbly before Him.

Spurgeon said, "What a blessing to be able to leave our matters in our surety's hands, knowing that all will be well, since He has an answer for every accuser, a rebuke for every reviler."

Surety is a covenant word. It's only by Jesus being our surety that we can be saved. We have no power deal with sin. It's only because He stands in our place that we can be saved. He is the surety of a better covenant (Heb. 7:22), and the one who guarantees the fulfillment of its promises.

Make my cause Thine own.
Let not the proud oppress me.
Leave me not alone.
Bind my heart and soul to Thee.

II. THE PSALMIST'S PASSIONATE
DESIRE VS.123-125

A. The Intensity Revealed v.123

My eyes fail from seeking Your salvation, and Your righteous word. The Psalmist has asked the Lord to be his surety in dealing with his haughty oppressors. Now he waits with great intensity of soul for the Lord's deliverance. His eyes are strained from looking and weeping until no tears are left. He used a similar expression in verses 81 and 82 where he speaks of his soul fainting and his eyes failing as he waits for the Lord's salvation.

He looks only to God. He doesn't seek deliverance from human resources. He knows his waiting will be rewarded. His surety is, "a God of justice; blessed are those who wait for Him" (Isa. 30:18).

It's like a company of soldiers surrounded by enemy forces. Help has been promised, but has not arrived. While they wait, they send a lookout to the highest hill to scan the horizon. The watchman looks and looks until his eyes are strained and dry.

Habakkuk brought his complaint before the Lord and said, "I will stand my watch and set myself upon the rampart and watch to see what He will say to me" (Hab.2:1). Then the Lord told him to write the vision and at the end it would speak and not lie. He said,

"Though it tarries, wait for it, because it will surely come; it will not tarry" (v.3).

The psalmist is looking for the truth of God's word to silence his oppressors. The haughty are humbled when the light of truth shines upon them. Today, the proud scorn us for holding to the truths of God's Word. We are called fools for believing God created the universe, that he sent His Son to save us, and that He is coming again. Like the psalmist, we yearn intensely for God's truth to vindicate us and glorify Him.

> Before Thee O Lord, I wait,
> For Thy salvation I pray.
> Please come and do not be late.
> I'm looking for Thee today.

B. The Instruction Requested. V.124

Deal with Your servant according to Your mercy, and teach me Your statutes. The word translated "deal" here, is the same word translated "done" in verse 121. The psalmist knew that even though he had done righteousness and justice, he still needed God's mercy. God's deliverances are always based on His mercy, not on the good we have done.

The psalmist's plea was that of a servant to his master. Ours is from a child to his father. Thank God, if a master will rescue his servant from oppressors, how much more will our heavenly Father have mercy on us and deliver us from our oppressors.

Experiencing God's mercy leads us to want to learn more about God's Word. Spurgeon said, "We may expect a master to teach his servants the meaning of his own orders. Yet, since our ignorance frequently arises from our own sinful stupidity, it is great mercy on God's part that He condescends to instruct us in His commandments."

The psalmist often repeats his request for teaching because he is aware again and again that he needs instruction in order to know and obey his master. Many times the deliverance we seek may come through a deeper understanding of God's Word.

> O Lord, have mercy on me,
> For without it I will fail,
> So to Thy Word I will flee,
> And by it I will prevail.

C. The Insight Required v.125

I am Your servant, give me understanding that I may know Your testimonies. This is the third time the psalmist has identified himself as a servant in this stanza. He seems to like the title, as did Jesus, who took upon Himself the form of a servant.

In the last verse he asked the Lord to teach him. In this one he asks for understanding. The word for understanding is *bign*, which means to discern or perceive. We can be taught and learn facts without understanding them. Knowledge comes through study, but understanding comes from God. Knowledge is of the mind, but understanding is of the heart.

Unbelievers have no understanding of the things of God, even though a few have some knowledge of them. Knowledge alone can blind the heart and lead to absurd conclusions because of darkened hearts. Some with great knowledge advocate wicked lifestyles with a passion because they don't know God or acknowledge the truth of His Word.

Understanding helps us to know God's will and purpose for our lives. The psalmist asked for understanding to help him deal with those who oppressed him. It will also help us deal with the difficult situations we face in life.

The Hebrew word for "know" is the very powerful word *yada* which means to have intimate knowledge of someone or something. It's used to describe the relationship between a man and his wife. The psalmist wants intimate knowledge of God. There he will find the truth he seeks. He will not be among those who are "ever learning, but never come to a knowledge of the truth" (II Tim. 3:7). Those who pursue an intimate knowledge of God and His Word will find the answers to life's questions. Casual readers may know its words, but not its secrets.

Upon me Thy wisdom bestow,
So that I might understand,
Teach me all that I need to know
To obey Thy every command.

III. THE PSALMIST'S PRESUMPTIOUS DEMAND V.126

A. His Daring v.126a

It is time for You to act, O Lord. The psalmist boldly asks God to assert His authority – to take action against his enemies. God has an appointed time for all His actions and He is never late. He told Habakkuk that the vision of judgment was for an appointed time. He had a time for sending His Son into the world, and He has a time for His return, a time which He alone knows.

If the times of God's actions are set, how can the psalmist declare that it's time for Him to act? Perhaps the answer is that those who are close to God's heart recognize the conditions which prompt God to act and boldly ask Him to intervene in the affairs of men. It was such a time when Joshua commanded the sun to stand still so that the battle might continue (Josh. 10:12-13). God even invites His people to command Him concerning His actions. "And concerning the work of My hands, you command me" (Isa. 45:11).

The psalmist doesn't name the actions he wants God to take. How God acts is left up to His own wisdom and power. He may act in ways contrary to what we would prescribe. Sometimes it's through providence and sometimes through miracles. At other times He may move by His Spirit on men's hearts, or raise up leaders to lead us..

Such praying is needed today. Our desperate times call for bold praying for God's intervention in the affairs of men.

B. His Discernment v.126b

For they have regarded Your law as void. He doesn't identify who "they" are. Perhaps they were the proud who oppress him. If so, his prayer isn't based on what they have done to him, but on their disregard for God's law. If they have disregarded God's law they have insulted the psalmist. David said, "The reproaches of those who reproach You have fallen on me" (Ps.69:9). However, the psalmist discerns that God will not just act to avenge those who have treated him badly. God will only act against those who break His law.

These lawbreakers disregard and defy God's law. They cast off all restraint. They call good evil, and evil good, and even deny the existence of right and wrong. To them there are only preferences or choices of lifestyles. Today we have "alternative lifestyles" and "women's choice." The Word of God is banned from our schools, and Christians are ridiculed for their faith. The church is corrupt and weak. Surely it is time for God to act!

O Lord, please act today,
For Thy law they make vain,
And Thy Word disobey
For their pleasure and gain.

IV. THE PSALMIST'S PRICELESS DISCOVERY VS.127-128

A. God's Word is Precious v.127

Therefore, I love Your commandments more than gold, yes, than fine gold. "Therefore" introduces us to a conclusion. It refers back to "They have regarded Your law as void" in the last verse. Because others made God's law void, the psalmist loves it all the more. Nothing will impress the believer more with the value of God's Word than to see the disobedience of those who consider it of no value.

Notice that it's the commandments he loves. It's easy to love the promises of blessing that encourage us, but it's more difficult to love the commandments that make demands on us.

Seeing others disregard and mock God's Word is even more reason for us to declare its truths and live by them. It's not the time to compromise or be silent.

The psalmist declared his love for the Word to be beyond his love for gold. Throughout history gold has fired men's imagination. They have made incredible sacrifices and endured great hardships to obtain it. Some have died for it, killed for it, even sold their souls for it. It has been the standard by which other things are valued. To the psalmist, the commandments of God were an even higher standard by which other things are measured.

A man was returning from the gold fields aboard a ship. He tied the gold he had mined in sacks around his waist. During the voyage the ship sank and the man was floundering in the water because of the weight of the gold. His fellow passengers, in life-boats only a few yards away, urged him to untie the bags of gold and swim to safety. Sadly, he loved his gold more than his life and he perished with it.

A miser who loves his treasure guards it and protects it with his life. He puts bars on his windows and buys a burglar alarm. God's Word is more precious than gold. The more men hate it the more we should guard its truths.

> I see the wicked rage
> And void Thy Words of old,
> But I love every page
> Above earth's finest gold.

B. God's Word is Perfect v.128

Therefore, all Your precepts concerning all things I consider to be right. I hate every false way. Here, we have the word "therefore" again which introduces the psalmist's second conclusion. In verse 127, he said he loves God's Word because it is rich. In this verse, he loves it because it is right. It's a treasure because it is truth.

The assessment given the Word by the world is wrong. The psalmist saw the wicked making God's law void, but he chose to place great value on it. In a day when the Word is being disregarded and even banished from public places, we would do well to follow his example.

The KJV says, "I esteem all Thy precepts." Esteem is probably a better translation of the Hebrew word *arak,* which means to put a value on something. It has a similar meaning to our word "appraise." The world assigns high values to things that have little real value. The assigned value of an item may relate to its rarity or to its relationship to a well-known person, such as a movie star, an athlete or a historical figure. I was reminded of this recently when I heard of a baseball card valued at $5,000. Jesus said, "For what is highly esteemed among men is an abomination in the sight of God" (Luke 16:15).

As Christians we place a high value on the Bible because we have a different value system. Once we rightly assess the value of God's Word, we are in a position to assign the right values to everything else. The Word is the standard by which all other things are valued. Jesus valued God's Word to be of greater value than food for the body, He said, "Man does not live by bread alone, but by every word that proceeds from the mouth of God" (Matt. 4:4). And Job said, "I have treasured the words of His mouth more than my necessary food" (Job 23:12).

The psalmist concluded that all of God's precepts concerning all things are right. Some say the Bible is right about spiritual things, but wrong about science and history. While the Bible is not primarily a history book or a science book, when it speaks of history or science, it is right. It's not right about some things, but about ALL THINGS – the things we like and the things we don't like. John Calvin said, "There is nothing to which we are more naturally inclined than to despise or reject whatever in God's law is disagreeable to us." We may try to avoid God's law, or disagree with it, but if we do, it is right and we are wrong.

The psalmist's love for the truth made him hate every false way – not some false ways, but EVERY false way. We need to seek out the false ways in our own hearts, in our homes and in our churches. If we consider all of God's Word to be right, all that is opposed to His Word is a false way.

God's Word is always right,
No matter what men may say.
It gives me truth and light,
So I hate every false way.

GOD'S WONDERFUL WORD

I. The Wonder of God's Word vs.129-132
   A. The Psalmist Lived by It v.129
   B. The Psalmist Learned from It v.130
   C. The Psalmist Longed for It vs.131-132
      1. The fervor he expressed v.131
      2. The favor he expected v.132
II. The Way of God's Word vs.133-136
   A. The Psalmist Was Blessed by It vs. 133-134
      1. He wanted direction v.133
      2. He wanted deliverance v.134
   B. The Psalmist Was Brightened by It v.135
   C. The Psalmist Was Burdened by It v.136

The psalmist's circumstances haven't changed. He's still oppressed by his enemies, yet he rejoices in the Word of God. The more he loves it, the richer it becomes. It's the stabilizing force in his troubled life.

I. THE WONDER OF GOD'S WORD
VS.129-132

A. The Psalmist Lived by It. v.129

Your testimonies are wonderful, therefore my soul keeps them. He literally says, "Your testimonies are wonders." They are a wonder to all who love them, study them and obey them. The more we study them with an obedient heart, the more we see their wonders.

Keep in mind that the testimonies, which the psalmist describes as wonders, were limited to the Law of Moses and perhaps a few Old Testament historical books. Today we have the full revelation of God in both the Old and New Testaments, and the knowledge of Him who is the Word made flesh (John 1:14). That makes His testimonies even more wonderful.

It sometimes takes a lifetime to realize that the so-called wonderful things of the world can't satisfy. As I write these words I'm 74 years old. I have seen many of the world's scenic wonders, which reflect God's glory. I've seen many of the marvels of man's work from the past – the pyramids of Egypt, the Parthenon in Athens, and the Colosseum in Rome and others. They were thrilling to see, but they offer no lasting satisfaction. The things of the world, no matter how wonderful they may seem, flash before our eyes and fade into memory, and sometimes from memory. But God's Word never loses its wonder. It's an inexhaustible fountain of delight.

The psalmist's obedience isn't a casual obedience. He says that his SOUL keeps God's testimonies. It's not motivated by the expectations of others, or the demands of his culture. Soul obedience flows from the heart.

Some study God's Word to obtain knowledge. Others may study it to impress others. The psalmist studied it to guide his daily life.

Lord, Thy Word exceeds
All the wonders of the earth.
So, let him who reads
Declare its infinite worth.

B. The Psalmist Learned from It. v.130

The entrance of Your word gives light; It gives understanding to the simple. The Hebrew word *petah*, translated "entrance" means to open up, to unfold or to reveal something. It's like opening a door to reveal what's inside. It's not just the Word entering the mind, but the unfolding of the Word so we can understand it. When its meaning is revealed to us it brings light.

Such unfolding or unveiling of the Word comes only from God. "For it is the God who commanded the light to shine out of darkness, who has shone in our hearts to give the light of the knowledge of the glory of God in the face of Jesus Christ" (II Cor.4:6).

The word "understanding" in this verse is the same word used in verse 125. In that verse the psalmist was praying for understanding. Here he tells us where it comes from and who can receive it. It comes from the unfolding or unveiling of God's Word, and it comes to the simple.

The simple are those who are open to it. For the Word to give light, it must be received with the simplicity of a child. David said in Psalm 19:7, "The testimony of the Lord is sure, making wise the simple." And in Psalm 25:9, he said, "The humble He guides in justice, and the humble He teaches His way." Jesus said, "I thank You Father, Lord of heaven and earth, that You have hidden these things from the wise and prudent and have revealed them unto babes" (Matt.11:25). We can understand God's Word only if we are teachable.

To keep God's Word from giving light, Satan tries to discredit the Bible, or take it out of the hands of those who are simple enough to be enlightened by it. To discredit it he raises up sophisticated scholars to deny its truth. To deny access to it he raises up sophisticated judges to make it illegal to read, or even display it in public school classrooms and in other public places.

Satan and his followers fear the Bible because they fear the light. They love darkness rather than light because their deeds are evil. When the light shines upon them they flee like bats to their caves at sunrise.

God's Word is a light
To the simple who believe,
And gives great delight
To all who its truth receive.

C. The Psalmist Longed for It vs. 131-132
   1. The fervor he expressed v.131

I opened my mouth and panted for I longed for Your commandments. The psalmist used the metaphor of a thirsty animal panting for the water to express his intense fervor of God's Word. David used the same metaphor in Psalm 41:1, when he said, "As the deer pants after the water brook, so pants my soul for You O God." Also, in Psalm 63:1, he said, "My soul thirsts for You; my flesh longs for You in a dry and thirsty land where there is no water."

As a deer pursued by hunters, finds refreshment in the cool water from a brook, so the psalmist, pursued by his oppressors, finds refreshment in the Word of God. Thirst is the most persistent and intense physical desire of both man and animal. We can't live more than a few days without water. The desire of the psalmist for God's Word was so intense that he compares it to thirst.

Many pant after the pleasures and possessions of the world, but few pant after God's Word. The world has nothing worth panting for. The things we need most in life are found in God's Word. Some pant after the gifts and blessings God can give, but few pant after the giver of all good gifts.

As I write this four baby robins are in their nest in a small tree just outside my window. Each time the mother robin returns with food the tiny birds open their mouths wide to receive it. They are not interested in the mother, only in the food she brings. I fear it's the same with many of us who come to God.

The word translated "longed" here is used nowhere else in the Old Testament. The psalmist used it to interpret the metaphor of panting. It means to desire earnestly. Notice that it's God's commandments that he longs for, not His comforts. Since he is oppressed by his enemies, to pray for comfort or deliverance would be understandable. But instead, his greatest desire is to obey God's commandments.

> As for water pants a deer,
> So for Thy Word I long.
> For it takes away my fear,
> And fills my heart with song.

2. The favor he expected v.132

Look upon me and be merciful to me, as Your custom is toward those who love Your name. First he longed for God's commandments, now the psalmist longs for His mercy. He doesn't ask for possessions or position. He asks only for mercy.

It's a prayer suitable for us all. We always need God's mercy, but sometimes we are more aware of our need than at others. There are times when we, like the psalmist, feel oppressed. It may be from people or circumstances. At other times it may arise out of our own weaknesses and limitations. In such times we can only cry out for mercy. When we're desperate we can be sure God sees us and knows our need and will hear our cries for mercy. If He knows the number of the hairs on our heads surely He knows every burden of our hearts.

The Lord delights in our cries for mercy. "The Lord takes pleasure in those that fear Him and those who hope in His mercy" (Ps.147:11). His mercies are never exhausted. Jeremiah said, "The Lord's mercies are not consumed, because His compassions fail not. They are new every morning" (Lam. 2:22-23). When the Lord sees us panting for His Word and crying out for mercy, He will hear us.

The psalmist prays that the Lord will be merciful to him just as has been His custom to be merciful in the past. He was encouraged by the many examples of God's mercy found in the Word.

We too can expect God to be merciful if we love His name. We can cry out as David did after his adultery with Bathsheba and murder of her husband, "Have mercy on me O God according to Your loving-kindness, according to the multitude of Your tender mercies, blot out my transgressions"(Ps.51:1).

Neither the nature nor the number of our sins can put us beyond the reach of God's mercy. We are never so far away that He cannot look upon us and hear our cries. One glance from His compassionate eye or one touch of His merciful hand can refresh our spirits and change our circumstances and remove the burden from our hearts.

O God, look upon me
And be merciful today,
As it's Thy nature to be
To all who Thy Word obey.

III. THE WAY OF GOD'S WORD VS.
133-136

A. The Psalmist was Blessed by It. vs. 133-134

1. He wanted direction v.133

Direct my steps by Your word, and let no iniquity have dominion over me. First, the psalmist wanted direction for walking according to the Word. The first impulse of the person who has experienced God's mercy is to obey His Word. He uses the Hebrew word *kun* again which is translated "direct" here. It's the same word translated "fashioned" in v.73. It means to design, establish or direct for a purpose. In verse 73, the psalmist said the Lord had fashioned or designed him for a purpose. Here he asks God to direct his steps according to God's Word. It's the word translated "ordered" in Psalm 37:23 where he said, "The steps of a good man are ordered by the Lord."

He wants his steps directed according to God's purpose as revealed in His Word, not according to a vision or a voice from heaven. He doesn't want to follow an impulse or a feeling. He not only wants to be on the right path, he wants his steps to be in harmony with God's Word. If he does, iniquity will not have dominion over him. Obedience to the Word breaks the power of evil over us. If we are dominated by the Word, we won't be dominated by evil.

The word "iniquity" carries the idea of nothingness, emptiness, futile pursuits and mischief. It includes not only things we might consider sinful, but things that are useless. There is danger that we will become so dominated by trivial things that we never accomplish anything worthwhile.

Direct my steps by Thy Word
And not by man's opinion,
That things evil and absurd,
Over me have no dominion.

2. He wanted deliverance v.134

Redeem me from the oppression of man, that I may keep Your precepts. The psalmist has repeatedly prayed for deliverance from his proud oppressors. Here he asks for redemption (deliverance or rescue) from the oppressions of man – a broader request.

Oppression can come from many sources. Sometimes it's from specific people. It may even come from members of our families. Unsaved husbands may oppress their Christian wives, putting great pressure on them contrary to their Christian convictions. Parents may oppress their Christian children in the same way.

Governments and leaders may oppress their people. It's true today, and it has always been true. The early Christians were oppressed by both Jews and Romans. Today, believers in China and Muslim countries are oppressed. American Christians are being oppressed by court rulings that limit their freedom of expression in public places.

Oppression can come from religious and educational authorities. Leaders of dominate churches, in some periods of history, have oppressed those who have disagreed with them. Many colleges and universities in America today oppress those who dissent from their teaching on homosexuality, evolution and abortion, and other liberal notions.

Oppression hinders obedience. The psalmist desires deliverance from oppression that he might be free to keep God's statutes. Oppression is wicked and it often drives men to wickedness. We need to ask the Lord how much of our faithfulness is due to our freedom from oppression. Would we be as faithful if we lived in China or in a Muslim country?

> Keep me from oppression.
> Let my soul be free
> To make a confession
> Of my love for Thee.

B. The Psalmist Was Brightened by It. v.135

Make Your face to shine upon Your servant. Teach me Your statutes. "Make Your face to shine," is an expression taken from the often repeated Jewish prayer found in Numbers 6:22-27. It is often quoted in the Psalms (See 31:6, 67:1, 80:3,7,14). It's a request for God to show His favor.

The psalmist isn't satisfied to just keep rituals and observe ceremonies. He is seeking God's smile upon his life. His oppressors have brought a cloud of darkness over him, but God's favor will brighten his life.

To be taught by the Lord is a sign of His favor. He never outgrew the need for God to teach him, nor do we. The more He favors us, the more we desire to learn His Word.

When I bow my knee
And look into His face,
In His smile I see
The glory of His grace.

C. The Psalmist Was Burdened by It v.136

Rivers of waters run down my eyes because men do not keep Your law. After praying for the light of God's face to shine upon him, the psalmist's face is now stained with tears. He asked God to teach him, so God taught him something about compassion for those who break His law. The psalmist felt indignation toward them in verse 55. In verse 120, he trembled over their fate. Now he weeps over them. His heart is clearly being conformed to the compassionate heart of God.

It's a burden he shared with Jeremiah who said, "O that I might weep day and night for the slain of the daughters of my people" (Jer.9:1). It also reminds us of the sorrow Paul felt for his fellow Jews when he said, "I have great sorrow and continual grief in my heart, for I could wish myself accursed from Christ for my brethren, my countrymen according to the flesh" (Rom.9:2-3).

Such concern must precede the salvation of the lost. However, it's a concern seldom seen today. There is little weeping so there is little reaping. The more we become like Christ, the more our hearts will be broken by the sins of those around us.

Today the Word of God is widely slandered in the media, on college campuses, and even in the pulpit. Its truths are ignored and its message called irrelevant.

Is it not time for rivers of water to flow from our eyes?

Give me eyes that weep
For those who against Thee sin,
And Thy law not keep,
Or heed the words therein.

STANZA 18: PSALM 119:137-144

GOD'S RIGHTEOUS WORD

I. His Description of God' Righteous Word vs.137-138
   A. The Righteousness of God's Character v.137
   B. The Righteousness of God's Commandments v.138

II. His Devotion to God's Righteous Word vs.139-141
   A. His Reason v.139
   B. His Response v.140
   C. His Remembrance v.141

III. His Delight in God's Righteous Word vs.142-144
   A. Because it is Everlasting v.142
   B. Because it is Encouraging v.143
   C. Because it is Enlightening v.144

No matter how he felt, no matter what his enemies did, or what his circumstances were, the psalmist stood firmly on God's righteousness and the truthfulness of His Word. His life was saturated with God's Word. He had no concordance or online commentaries or other sources of instant information. His knowledge came from hours and hours of searching, reading, memorizing and meditation. This led him to the deep convictions he expressed in this stanza.

I. HIS DESCRIPTION OF GOD'S RIGHTEOUS WORD VS.137-138

A. The Righteousness of God's Character v.137

Righteous are You O Lord, and upright are your judgments. It's rare that the psalmist uses God's name as he does here. As he thinks of God's perfect righteousness, he worships in awe. God's righteousness is often extolled in the Psalms. For example, "The Lord is righteous in all His ways, gracious in all His works" (145:17).

It the Old Testament God's righteousness often stood in contrast to Israel's sinfulness. "O Lord God of Israel, You are righteous, for we are left a remnant, as it is this day. Here we are before You in our guilt, though no one can stand before You because of this" (Ezra 9:13)! Daniel expresses the same truth, "O Lord, righteousness belongs to You, but to us shame of face, as it is this day, to the men of Judah because of the unfaithfulness which they have committed against You" (Dan. 9:7).

The chasm between God's perfect righteousness and man's sinfulness can only be bridged by Jesus Christ who took our sin upon Himself that we might become righteous through Him. He is "the Lord our righteousness" (Jer. 23:6).

Although he is often perplexed and distressed, the psalmist knows a righteous God will always do right. In the short term he may not always understand. Yet he knows in the end, God will make all things right. That knowledge comforts him, and is a powerful principle to guide his life, and ours.

If God is righteous, His judgments are always right. The psalmist doesn't separate God's righteousness from His righteous Word. What the Word says about God is true, and what God says in His Word is true. David said, "The judgments of the Lord are true and righteous altogether" (Ps. 19:9).

When what the world says differs from what God says, God is right and the world is wrong. The world calls homosexuality an alternative lifestyle. The Bible calls it an abomination. The world says life evolved out of slime. The Bible says God created it. The world calls sex outside of marriage acceptable. The Bible calls it sin. The Bible is right and the world is wrong.

Several carpenters were cutting boards for a construction project. One man was measuring the end of each board with a T-square to see if the cut was exactly 90 degrees. If it wasn't, it had to be cut again. God's Word is the T-square by which all truth is measured. If an idea doesn't square with what the

Bible says, it's the idea that needs to be changed, not the Bible.

Those who defy a righteous God and deny His Word may prosper in the short term, but they will eventually be judged by God's standards. Jeremiah said, "Righteous are You O Lord, when I plead with You: Yet let me talk with You about Your judgments. Why does the way of the wicked prosper? Why are those happy who deal so treacherously" (Jer. 12:1)? His conclusion was that they were like sheep being led to the slaughter and didn't know their final end.

If there is a dispute between you and God, you can be sure that God is right and you are wrong. If others have treated you unfairly, you can be assured that God will make it right.

> Our God is righteous and true.
> His Word can never be broken.
> He will all evil subdue,
> And fulfill all He has spoken.

B. The Righteousness of His Commandments v.138

Your testimonies which You have commanded are righteous and very faithful. David said, "The law of the Lord is perfect, converting the soul; the testimony of the Lord is sure, making wise the simple; the statutes of the Lord are right, rejoicing the heart; the commandment of the Lord is pure, enlightening the eyes" (Ps. 19:7-8).

God's Word deserves our confidence, and is worthy of our trust. It will never fail. Spurgeon said,

"His testimonies are righteous and may be relied on for the present; they are faithful and may be trusted for the future. For about every portion of the inspired word there is a divine authority for they are published by God's command."

God's testimonies are righteous and "very faithful," meaning they are exceedingly or abundantly faithful. They will never mislead us. God is faithful to what He has spoken and not one word will ever be broken.

Our laws are made by flawed people with their own agendas. They may also be influenced by others who have their special interests. But God's laws are just. He's not influenced by the opinions of men. He's not running for office, or trying to gain the approval of men. He's interested only in righteousness and truth.

God's Word is without flaw,
And all He says will be.
Very faithful is his law
That daily comforts me.

II. HIS DEVOTION TO GOD'S RIGHTEOUS WORD VS.139-141

A. His Reason v.139

My zeal has consumed me because my enemies have forgotten Your word. The word "zeal" means intense passion or fervor. It can be a combination of anger, love and sorrow. David said in Psalm 69:9, "The zeal of Your house has eaten me up." Jesus quoted this verse when He drove the money changers out of the Temple (John 2:17). The psalmist's zeal consumed him. It overwhelmed him and exhausted him.

The reason for the psalmist's passion was that his enemies had forgotten God's Word. He felt indignation for them in verse 55. In verse 120, he trembled over their fate. In verse 136, he wept for them. Now his passion for them burns in his heart. It's not because they are his enemies and want to destroy him; it's because they have forgotten God's Word. If they have forgotten it, it means that they must have heard it. He was so passionate for it that he was overwhelmed to think anyone would forget it.

Why would anyone forget anything so faithful and true as God's Word? We might ask that question in our own time. Why has our nation so neglected and forgotten the Bible? How do you feel when you see the Word of God mocked and marginalized by the enemies of God? Does it set our hearts ablaze? Does it ignite a zeal for it in us?

> Lord, set my heart ablaze
> When men forget Thy Word,
> And walk not in Thy ways,
> As if they've never heard.

B. His Response v.140

Your word is very pure, therefore, Your servant loves it. The psalmist responds to the forgetfulness of his enemies by loving God's Word even more. Ten times in this psalm the writer declares his love for God's Word. Here, he says he loves it because of its purity. It's not so with man's word. Our nature is tainted by sin, so our words reflect our nature. God's Word also reflects His nature. His Word is pure because He is pure. It's not only pure, but very pure. It's like silver and gold that has been refined over and over. "The words of the Lord are pure words, like silver tried in a furnace of earth seven times, purified seven times" (Ps. 12:6). Also, "Every word of God is pure" (Prov.30:5).

God's words are not only pure truth, they are pure light. We can love them without limit and obey them without reservation. They will do us no harm. Since they are pure, they will purify our hearts.

The writings of men are flawed because we are both limited and sinful. About 25 years ago I wrote my first book. If I would write the same book now it would be vastly different because my understanding of the subject is greater today. That's not so with God's book. It is perfect and will never need to be updated.

Men love and hate God's Word for the same reason – because it is pure. Those with pure hearts love it, but those with sinful hearts hate it because its words condemn them. No one can love sin and love the Word.

I know Thy Word is pure
For every word you did inspire.
It will always endure
And to love it is my desire.

C. His Remembrance v.141

I am small and despised, yet I do not forget Your precepts. The word translated "small" here can mean few in number, young in age, small in size or low in rank or esteem. In this context it probably means lowly in his own sight. To be despised is to be treated unworthy of notice, or looked upon with contempt because of rank, poverty, age, education or religion.

The world measures us by education, accomplishments, wealth, position and social standing. God has a different yardstick. Those least esteemed by men may be the greatest in God's sight. Paul was "made the filth of the world, the offscouring of all things" (I Cor. 4:13). If we make God's Word our manual for daily living we are likely to be scorned by those in high worldly positions.

Paul was not only considered to be the filth of the world by others, he considered himself to be "the least of all saints" (Eph. 3:8). To be small in our own eyes and scorned by others helps us remember God's Word and to rely on it as the psalmist did. It helps us rise above the smallness and scorn.

We don't know who wrote this psalm, but this verse certainly describes David's condition during the years he was pursued by Saul. His band was few in number, and he was despised and hunted like an animal, yet he never forgot God's Word.

Although I am weak and small,
And by every man despised,
I remember Thy precepts all,
For they are highly prized.

III, HIS DELIGHT IN GOD'S
RIGHTEOUS WORD VS.142-144

A. Because it is Everlasting v.142

Your righteousness is an everlasting righteousness, and Your law is truth. All God says and does is right because God is righteous. That has always been true and it always will be because God's righteousness is everlasting. "For I am the Lord, I do not change' (Mal.3:6).

What was right for past generations is right for this generation and it will be right for the next generation. Men may redefine right and wrong to cover their sins, but God's definition never changes. Nor does his righteousness change with our circumstances. It's the same when we are sick as when we are healthy. It's the same when we are poor as it is when we are rich. No matter what our circumstances are, God will always do the right thing.

Because God is righteous, He preserves and delivers the righteous. God said to Noah, "Come into the Ark, you, and all your household, because I have seen that you are righteous before me in this generation" (Gen. 7:1). Peter describes Noah as "a preacher of righteousness" (II Peter 2:5). He also said that He delivered Lot, a righteous man whose soul was vexed with the words and actions of the wicked (vs.7-8).

We don't achieve righteousness by keeping rules and conforming to certain standards of behavior. The Pharisees were experts at keeping rules, but Jesus said, "For I say unto you, unless your righteousness exceeds the righteousness of the Scribes and

Pharisees, you will by no means enter the kingdom of heaven" (Matt.5:20).

Our righteousness is not sufficient. We must put on God's righteousness. That has always been true, and it's still true today. We can only receive God's righteousness by faith. "Abraham believed God and it was accounted unto him for righteousness" (Rom. 4:3). Paul also said, "With the heart one believes unto righteousness and with the mouth confession is made unto salvation" (Rom. 10:10).

As God is perfect righteousness, so His law is perfect truth. Jesus affirmed this when He said in His prayer for the disciples in John 17:17, "Sanctify them by Your truth. Your word is truth." Like His righteousness, God's truth never changes. Jesus said, "Till heaven and earth pass away, one jot or tittle will by no means pass from the law till all is fulfilled" (Matt.5:18).

In his "Treasury of David," Spurgeon quotes the Puritan writer Thomas Manton, pointing out that God's Word is 1, The chief truth. All the writings of man may contain truth, but they are only fragments and scraps of truth. 2. It is the only truth that reveals the mind of God. 3. It is pure truth. In it there is no mixture of falsehood, and 4. It is the whole truth. It contains everything necessary for salvation.

Those who base their lives on God's Word are living lives based on reality. The lifestyles of the world are based on illusions. God's Word is an unerring guide for living. Those who live by it will never lose their way.

Thy righteousness forever stands,
And Thy Word is always true,
So I obey all Thy commands
And give Thee all honor due.

B. Because it is Encouraging v.143

Trouble and anguish have overtaken me, yet Your commandments are my delight. The word "trouble" can refer to any kind of affliction. The psalmist doesn't reveal the nature of his trouble, but since he has often referred to his oppressors, we may assume he is referring to them.

Anguish means being pressed or compressed. It's the inner stress that comes from the troubles we face. Paul spoke of his external troubles in II Corinthians 1:8, "For we do not want you to be ignorant, brethren, of our trouble which came to us in Asia, that we were burdened above measure and above strength, so that we despaired even of life." And in II Corinthians 7:5, he speaks, not only of his troubles, but of his fears. "We are troubled on every side. Outside were conflicts, inside were fears."

The word for "taken hold of me," is the Hebrew word *masa* which means to be pursued and found, as being chased by hounds and caught. Trouble and anguish have caught up with the psalmist. They are in constant pursuit of us all, and will find us sooner or later. Job said, "Man who is born of woman is of few days and full of trouble" (Job 14:1).

The psalmist is distressed, yet he is delighted. It's the Word, not the world, that brings delight in the time of trouble. The Bible isn't a trouble repellant, but it's a source of strength when trouble catches up with us. It not only gives us strength, it brings us joy. Sometimes our strength comes from our joy. Nehemiah said, "The joy of the Lord is your strength" (Neh. 8:10).

James declares that trials are a reason for rejoicing, "Brethren, count it all joy when you fall into various trials, knowing that the trial of your faith produces patience" (James 1:2). Our trials are only temporary, but the Word of God is eternal. Paul said, "For our light affliction, which is but for a moment, is working for a far more eternal weight in glory" (II Cor. 4:1). Peter echoes the same truth, "In this you greatly rejoice, though now for a little while, if need be, you have been grieved by various trials" (I Peter 1:6).

It's not God's promises of victory that give the psalmist joy, but His commandments. It's not just hearing the Word of God, but obeying it that delights him. David said, "I delight to do Your will O my God, and Your law is within my heart" (Ps. 40:8).

In time of trouble and stress, hold fast to God's Word and obey it, no matter what the circumstances are. Daniel was under great stress when he had to choose between obedience to God and being thrown to the lions. He continued to obey God's commandments, and was thrown to the lions, but God delivered him. Trouble is never and excuse for disobedience.

> In Thy Word I delight
> When my troubles are intense.
> It's my song in the night
> And is my greatest defense.

C. Because it is Enlightening v.144

The righteousness of Your testimonies is ever-lasting; give me understanding and I shall live. The psalmist said that God's testimonies are righteous in verse 138, then, in verse 142, he says His righteousness is everlasting. Now he says that the righteousness of God's testimonies are everlasting. He is giving us an expanded and more detailed explanation as he goes forward. He ties righteousness to the Word and shows it to be everlasting.

His righteous testimonies are not only the standard of righteousness for the Jews, but also for the gentiles. They are not just the standard for one generation, but for every generation. They are not just the standard for one situation, but for all situations. They don't require any adjustments or alterations to fit the different circumstances of life. They are the standard of righteousness for all people in every place and at every time.

As he has done many times before, the psalmist prays for understanding. New situations in life don't require a new revelation from God, but they may require a new understanding of the revelation we already have. Here the psalmist is asking for understanding to deal with his troubles. The prayer for understanding is a prayer we all pray when troubles come. Solomon said, "Happy is the man who finds wisdom and the man who gains understanding" (Prov.3:13). He also advises, "In all your getting, get understanding" (Prov.4:7).

Thy Word is always right
In every day and age.
May I walk in the light
That shines from every page.

STANZA 19: PSALM 119:145-152

A CRY FOR HELP

I. The Psalmist's Cry vs.145-148
    A. His Cries Were Fervent v.145
    B. His Cries Were Focused v.146
    C. His Cries Were Frequent v.147-148
        1. He meets with God in the morning v.147
        2. He meditates on God's Word at midnight v.148
II. The Psalmist's Call vs.149-150
    A. His Simple Plea v.149
    B. His Serious Problem v.150
III. The Psalmist's Comfort vs.151-152
    A. The Nearness of God v.151a
    B. The Nature of God's Word vs.151b-152
        1. It is true v.151b
        2. It is timeless v.152

In this stanza the psalmist gives us a picture of his prayer life. He tells us how he prays, when he prays, what he prays for and the basis upon which he makes his requests. It's a powerful lesson on prayer for us.

I. THE PSALMIST'S CRY VS.145-148

A. His Cries Were Fervent v.145

I cry out with my whole heart; Hear me, O lord! I will keep Your statutes. The psalmist's cry comes from deep within him. Prayers from the heart are both fervent and sincere. God is not concerned about the right form, the right words, the length, or the loudness of our prayers. He wants to hear the fervent cries of our hearts. James says, "The effectual fervent prayer of a righteous man avails much" (James 5:16).

John Bunyan said, "When thou prayst, rather let your heart be without words than thy words be without heart." Thomas Morton said, "There is no reality in prayer, whatever be in it, if the heart is not in it." Thomas Brooks said, "If the heart be dumb, God will certainly be deaf." Charles Spurgeon said, "Heart cries are the essence of prayer."

The psalmist cries out with his whole heart. His whole being is focused on his desire. No halfhearted prayers will reach the throne of God.

He cried out. His cry originated in his heart, but it passed through his lips on its way to heaven. The words "cry out," are used in other places to indicate an intense, even desperate cry. It was the cry of the desperate sailors in the storm-tossed ship with Jonah aboard, and of Jonah in the belly of the fish (Jonah 1:13, 2:2). David uses it in Psalm 34:6, when he writes, "This poor man cried out, and the Lord heard him and saved him out of all his troubles."

In his book, "The Power of Crying Out," Bill Gothard points out the difference between crying out and our usual kind of praying. He says God may allow a situation to become so hopeless that we can do nothing to solve the problem. So we cry out to God in our total inability do anything. When we do, sometimes the answer comes immediately.

The psalmist isn't satisfied just to pray. He wants to be heard, and he asks the Lord to hear him. He's not like the Sunday school class who wrote to a missionary saying, "We wanted you to know that we are praying for you. We don't expect an answer." If God doesn't hear and answer our prayers, we pray in vain.

He attaches a promise to keep God's statutes to his prayer. He doesn't expect God to hear and answer his cry unless he's willing to hear God's Word and obey it.

This kind of desperate fervent prayer is greatly needed today but seldom practiced. Ron Dunn, said, "The trouble is that our situation is desperate, but we are not." When we in desperation cry out for revival, it will come. When we desperately cry out for souls, they will be saved. May we be as desperate as John Knox who cried out, "O God, give me Scotland or I die."

Lord, let Thine ear draw nigh;
Listen to my earnest plea.
Hear my desperate cry;
Extend Thy mercy to me.

B. His Cries Were Focused v.146

I cry out to You; save me, and I will keep Your testimonies. Again the psalmist cried out. He is still fervent, but now his cries are more focused. In verse 145, he asks God to hear him. Now he asks God to save him. In verse 145, we see how he prayed. Here we have what he prayed for.

He doesn't say what he needs to be saved from, but it doesn't matter. God knew and he knew. He has earlier spoken of his afflictions, of the dangers that surrounded him, of his enemies who pursued him and the proud who oppressed him. Perhaps he is praying for deliverance from all of these.

We are in constant need of deliverance from the dangers we face in our daily walk – the temptations that beset us, the devil who accuses us and the trials that test us. Even when our troubles are of our own making, we can still cry out for God's help.

His prayer is short and to the point. Fervent prayers are never wordy. He simply cried, "Save me." He uses no flowery words. He doesn't quote promises from the Bible or shape his prayer into an acceptable theological formula. David wrote in Psalm 55:16, "As for me, I will call upon God and the Lord will save me."

Again, he attaches a promise to his prayer. He said, "I will keep Your testimonies." It isn't clear whether he is promising to keep God's testimonies if he is delivered, or he can only keep them if he is delivered. In either case, his promise of obedience is tied to his cry. This is not a "foxhole" prayer that makes rash promises to obey God if He will rescue him from a dangerous situation. It's a firm resolve repeated from the previous verse for emphasis.

I cry out to Thee;
Rescue me today.
Set Thy servant free
Thy Word to obey.

C. His Cries Were Frequent vs.147-148
  1. He meets with God in the morning. v.147

I arise before the dawning of the morning and cry for help; I hope in Your word. The psalmist was up before the sun, pleading his cause before the Lord while the dew was still on the grass. David said, "My voice shall You hear in the morning. O Lord, in the morning I will direct it to You and look up" (Ps.5:3). He also said, "To You I have cried out O Lord, and in the morning my prayer comes to You" (Ps.88:13). Jesus too, arose to pray early in the morning."Having risen a long while before daylight, He went out and departed to a solitary place; and there He prayed" (Mark 1:35-36).

We get up early to shop for bargains, to stand in line for concert or sporting event tickets, to go hunting or fishing or to get an early start on a trip. Why then, is it so hard for us to get up early to pray?

It's the third time the psalmist cried out to God. Jesus prayed three times in the garden for the cup of His suffering to be removed. Paul prayed three times for God to remove the thorn in his flesh. Fervent prayer is persistent prayer. Elijah prayed seven times for rain before the cloud appeared.

Hope based on the promises of God's Word kept the psalmist praying. Hope is a powerful motivator for prayer. We wouldn't pray if we had no hope that God will hear and answer us. Perhaps as he prayed, the rising of the morning sun reminded him of faithfulness and renewed his hope every morning.

> I'm up before the day
> While darkness shrouds the land.
> So cast me not away,
> For on Thy Word I stand.

2. He meditates on God's Word at midnight v.148

My eyes are awake through the night watches that I may meditate on Your word. The night was divided into three watches. At the end of each watch, the guards who kept watch over the city, changed. The psalmist lay awake in the night anticipating the changing of the guard. He used the time when he was awake to meditate on God's Word. What do you think about when you are awake in the night?

May we follow Paul's advice to redeem the time because the days are evil (Eph. 5:16). While he was in the Judean wilderness, David wrote, "When I remember You upon my bed, I meditate on You in the night watches" (Ps. 62:6).

The psalmist has already mentioned meditation six times in this psalm, so there's no need to repeat what we have already said about it. The Word was already hidden in his mind and close to his heart, so he used every opportunity to call it up and chew on it. Spurgeon said, "Meditation was the food of his hope, and the solace of his sorrow. It is instructive to find meditation so constantly connected with fervent prayer; it is the fuel which sustains the flame."

When awake in the night
Thy Word is on my mind,
And when my soul is quiet
Great peace in it I find.

II. THE PSALMIST'S CALL VS.149-150

A. His Simple Plea v.149

Hear my voice according to Your lovingkindness. O Lord, revive me according to Your justice. The psalmist's prayer continues, but in a calmer spirit. His desperate cries have become a more reasoned prayer based on the nature of God and the promises of His covenant. As we have already pointed out, lovingkindness includes both God's favor and His faithfulness. David speaks of it as the source of our forgiveness, our healing, our redemption and the source of all God's benefits (See Ps. 103:1-5).

God doesn't hear us because of our goodness. We don't receive His benefits because we deserve them, but because of God's lovingkindness. Because of it,

God overlooks the imperfections of our prayers and our failures, and gives us more than we ask or think.

The psalmist asks God to hear him based on His lovingkindness and to answer him based on His justice. The word translated "justice" is *mispat*, which is sometimes translated judgment. The idea seems to be fairness, or what is right, or according to God's sovereign wisdom.

The psalmist has already prayed to be revived several times. Now he has been crushed by oppression, distress, afflictions and even depression. He seems to be asking God to renew his vigor and strength, and his relationship with God. It is similar to the words of Psalm 71:20, "You, who have shown me great and severe troubles, shall revive me again and raise me up from the depths of the earth."

> To me Thine ear incline
> According to Thy goodwill.
> Restore this life of mine,
> And continue with me still.

B. His Serious Problem v.150

They draw near who follow after wickedness. They are far from Your law. Evil men are never far from the psalmist. In the past they have lied about him, slandered him, set traps for him and oppressed him. They never let up. They're not content with just doing their evil deeds and letting other people alone. They want to unleash evil against those who want to do good.

They are near to the psalmist, but they are far from God's law. They are not under its influence. Those who do evil despise God's Word. They don't want to obey it, nor do they want others to be influenced by it. They don't want the 10 Commandments to be posted in public places or the Bible to be in classrooms.

The Word of God was a powerful influence in the lives of the founders of our nation. For nearly 200 years that influence continued. But now, we've drifted far from God's law, and our culture shows it. There is no longer any absolute truth or distinction between good and evil. Those who not only follow after wickedness, but actively promote it are not far from any one of us. Their influence seeps into our homes through television. Their words are printed in almost every magazine and newspaper. Their sounds are heard in our music, and their lifestyles are portrayed in our movies. Some teach our children and grandchildren in our schools.

> As wicked men draw near,
> Who follow not Thy ways,
> Their evil intent is clear
> As upon me they gaze.

III. THE PSALMIST'S COMFORT
VS.151-152

A. By the Nearness of God v.151a
You are near O Lord. Wicked men are near, but the Lord is nearer. That's all the comfort the psalmist

needs. If God was near he had no fear of evil men. "The Lord is near to all who call upon Him, to all who call upon Him in truth" (Ps.145:18). And Isaiah said, "He is near who justifies me; who will contend with me" (Isa. 50:8). When God is near fear vanishes. "I will not be afraid of tens of thousands of people who have set themselves against me all around" (Ps. 3:6).

In her book, "The Christian's Secret of a Happy Life," Hannah Whitall Smith tells of a woman who had a vision in which she was surrounded by a great light. A voice told her the light was the presence of God. Then dreadful things passed before her – fighting armies, wicked men, raging beasts, storms, pestilence, sin and suffering of every kind. At first she reacted with terror. Then she saw she was so surrounded by the presence of God that nothing could touch her unless God allowed it.

We too, should be greatly comforted by knowing that God's presence protects us from those who would harm us. God told Isaiah, "Fear not, for I am with you. Be not dismayed for I am your God. I will strengthen you. Yea, I will help you. I will uphold you with my righteous right hand. Behold, all those who are incensed against you shall be ashamed and disgraced. They shall be as nothing" (Isa.41:10-11).

B. By the Nature of God's Word vs.151b-152
  1. God's Word is truth v.151b
    All Your commandments are truth. God's truth will prevail. God's commandments are not only true, they ARE truth – the truth by which all things are

measured. God's presence and God's truth were the psalmist's only defense against the mischief-makers who wanted to harm him.

> Thy presence and truth protect me
> From those who mischief make.
> They submit not their wills to Thee,
> Nor their evil ways forsake.

2. God's Word is timeless v.152

Concerning Your testimonies, I have known of old that You have established them forever. The expression "of old" in the Old Testament means something passed down from previous generations as in Psalm 44:1, "We have heard with our ears, O God. Our fathers have told us, the deeds You did in their days, in days of old." Isaiah said, "O Lord, You are my God. I will exalt You. I will praise Your name. For You have done wonderful things. Your counsels of old are faithful and true" (Isa.25:1).

The psalmist isn't seeking comfort in some new thing. He will stick with what has been established and proven true by many generations.

James M. Boyce tells about a mechanic who was called to repair a large telescope. During the lunch hour, an astronomer came by and saw the man reading his Bible. "Why are you reading that?" he asked. "The Bible is out of date. You don't even know who wrote most of it." The mechanic replied, "You make use of the multiplication tables to make calculations in your work don't you?" "Of course," answered the astronomer. "Do you know who wrote them?" the mechanic asked. "I suppose not," the astronomer said. "Then how can you trust them?" the mechanic responded. "Because they work," answered the astronomer. "Well, I trust the Bible for the same reason – it works," The mechanic answered.

Not only have God's testimonies been reliable in the past, they will continue to be reliable in the future. "Forever, O Lord, Your Word is settled in heaven" (v.89). Man's version of truth may change because our knowledge is incomplete. But God is not lacking in knowledge. He doesn't get any new revelation or discover any new truth. His truth is complete so it never changes.

That knowledge keeps the psalmist's feet on a firm path when the wicked are nipping at his heels. He has no place for political correctness that embraces many versions of the truth. Nor does he seek out science or scholarship to find out what truth is. He wants the truth that is as old as the hills and as fixed as the mountains. He clings to the truth of God's Word that is from old and will remain forever. Zemek says, "God's decrees represent a more enduring dimension of reality than the psalmist's present experience." He looks beyond his temporary troubles and finds comfort in God's eternal truth.

> Thy Word is settled of old.
> On it I can depend.
> Its truth has often been told,
> And it shall have no end.

STANZA 20: PSALM 119:153-160

DEALING WITH AFFLICTION

I. The Psalmist's Condition vs.153-156
   A. He Prays for an Acknowledgment v.153
   B. He Pleads for an Advocate v.154
   C. He Prepares an Argument v.155
   D. He Presents an Appeal v.156
II. The Psalmist's Critics vs.157-158
   A. They are Many v.157
   B. They are Misguided v.158
III. The Psalmist's Confidence vs.159-160
   A. Based on God's Tender Ways v.159
   B. Based on God's Truthful Words v.160
      1. It is entirely true v.160a
      2. It is eternally true v.160b

The psalmist refers to his afflictions more than 50 times in this psalm. They include persecution, oppression, slander, loneliness, and many unidentified troubles. The last stanza began with a desperate cry for help. But after meditating on God's Word, he became calmer and found comfort. In this stanza he presents his case to the Lord as an attorney would present a case to a judge. We are reminded of the words of Job in his time of suffering, "I would present my case before Him, and fill my mouth with arguments" (Job 23:4).

I. THE PSALMIST'S CONDITION
VS.152-156

A. He Prays for an Acknowledgement v.153

Consider my affliction and deliver me, for I do not forget Your law. He believes he has a good case and wants a hearing before God. He wants the Lord to weigh his arguments and render a decision. In our country, before one can get the Supreme Court's decision on a matter, the court must agree to hear the case. The psalmist is asking for a hearing of his case. He believes that if the Lord will hear his case He will deliver him from his afflictions.

He strengthens his appeal by reminding the Lord of his obedience to His law. His afflictions are not the result of his breaking God's law. He is a loyal obedient servant, not one who has disregarded the law and ignored His commandments.

I make my plea to Thee
That Thou might hear my case,
And issue Thy decree
To save me from disgrace.

B. He Pleads for an Advocate v.154

Plead my case and redeem me; Revive me according to Your word. The psalmist's troubles had become too great for him to handle. He needed someone to deal with them on his behalf, someone to take away his burden. A few years ago I had some legal issues with the government. Since I had no ability to deal with the issues, I had to hire an attorney to do it for me. The psalmist was asking the Lord to be his attorney and defend him against those who persecuted him.

In Psalm 35:1, David wrote, "Plead my cause, O Lord, with those who strive against me, fight against those who fight against me." He prayed a similar prayer in Psalm 43:1, "Vindicate me O God, and plead my cause against an ungodly nation; O deliver me from the deceitful and unjust man."

The psalmist asks the Lord to plead his cause and redeem him. The word "redeem" used here is used to describe a kinsman redeemer who redeems his next of kin from slavery or poverty. When the Israelites were being oppressed and taken into captivity by their enemies, Jeremiah said, "Their redeemer is strong: the Lord of Hosts is His name. He will thoroughly plead their cause" (Jer. 50:34). We can take comfort in God's promise that the Lord will take up our cause and intervene on our behalf.

The psalmist calls on the Lord to "revive" him 11 times in this psalm. Three of them are in this stanza. Troubles drain the life from us over time, not only spiritually, but mentally and physically as well. We all need to be refreshed and revived on a regular basis. The psalmist's troubles seemed extreme, so he asks God for a new infusion of strength again and again.

He asks the Lord to represent him, to redeem him and revive him, all according to God's Word.

> O Lord, stand by my side
> And be my advocate.
> Unto Thee I have cried,
> For my troubles are great.

C. He Prepares an Argument v.155

Salvation is far from the wicked, for they do not seek Your statutes. At first glance this verse may not appear to be an argument. However, it seems to me the psalmist wants to distinguish between himself and the wicked who persecute and oppress him. He seeks God's Word, loves it and keeps it. His persecutors, who bring accusations against him, do not.

One of the tactics of a defense attorney is to try to impeach the character of those who bring charges against his client. It's useless for evil men to bring charges against the righteous in the court of heaven. They have no standing before God and no grounds for their actions against the child of God.

Not only that, they have no knowledge of the statutes by which God renders His judgments. They don't seek His statutes or understand His laws. They, themselves, are gross violators of them. They have no advocate to plead their cause against the righteous.

A few years before I am writing this, an atheist in California filed suit to remove the words "under God" from the pledge of allegiance to the flag. The case went all the way to the United States Supreme Court. However, the Supreme Court refused to hear the case because the man who filed the suit had no standing in the case. That is, he had no basis for filing the suit because he had suffered no harm by the words.

So the psalmist's plea is that his accusers have no grounds for accusing him before God. When Satan, our accuser, brings accusations against us let us remember that Jesus' death on the cross cleared us of all charges, Therefore, Satan has no grounds for bringing any accusations against us.

> The wicked ignore Thy commands,
> And before Thee have no claim
> Against those now held in Thy hands,
> And called by Thy holy name.

D. He Presents an Appeal v.156

Great are Your tender mercies, O Lord; Revive me according to Your judgments. The psalmist bases his plea on God's great and tender mercies. The word translated "great" means many in number and in form. They are not only many, but of great variety. There are mercies to cover every need.

In Psalm 69:16, David, wrote, "Turn to me according to the multitude of Your tender mercies."

Also included is the idea that God's mercies are so extensive that they are available to all men. "The Lord is good to all, and His tender mercies are over all His works" (Ps.145:9).

The word "tender" is often used to describe God's mercies. It means to be tender as young plant as opposed a hardened tree. It describes His responsiveness to our needs. His mercies are as fresh and tender as a new plant and they last forever (See Psalm 136).

The mercy the psalmist was seeking was for revival after being beaten down by persecution and oppression. He asked for it according to God's judgments, not according to his own feelings. All God's mercies come to us according to the promises, principles and precepts of God's Word.

To Thee O God, I plead,
Just as I've done before.
Grant mercy for my need,
And my strength restore.

II. THE PSALMIST'S CRITICS
VS.157-158

A. They are Many v.157

Many are my persecutors and enemies, yet I do not turn from Your testimonies. The psalmist needs many mercies because he has many enemies. His persecutors will never outnumber God's mercies. He is like a fox pursued by a pack of hounds. We can't expect to live holy lives without being pursued by unholy men. Jesus told the 12, "If the world hates you, know that it hated me before it hated you" (John 15:18). Paul said, "All who desire to live godly in Christ Jesus will suffer persecution" (II Tim.3:12). David said in Psalm 34:19, "Many are the afflictions of the righteous, but the Lord delivers him out of them all."

The word "many" implies not only many in number but many in kind. The psalmist's many persecutors attacked him in many different ways. The more numerous and varied our enemies, the more pressure they exert on us.

The Hebrew word translated "turn" here is *natah*. It's used to describe Solomon's heart being turned away after other gods by his foreign wives in his old age. One wife may not have put much pressure on him, but many caused him to yield. The more persecutions we face the more difficult it is to remain faithful. Each enemy attacks us in a different way, and each trial exerts some new pressure on us.

If our enemies fail to divert us from obedience to God's Word, they fail in their mission. David said in Psalm 44:18, "Our heart has not turned back, nor have our steps departed for Your way." May it be so with us, no matter how many or varied the attacks against us.

They have pursued me from my youth,
And their numbers still increase.
Yet, I will not turn from Thy truth,
Nor my hold on Thy Word release.

B. They are Misguided v.158

I see the treacherous and am disgusted because they do not keep Your word. The psalmist has repeatedly voiced his disgust for those who don't obey God's Word (See vs. 53,126,136). The word "treacherous" is used in other places to describe those who are unfaithful to their covenants, such as marriage (See Mal. 2:10-14). Here they are traitors who break God's Word.

The word "disgusted" is a translation of *qut* which means to feel revulsion toward something. It's used by Job in Job 10:1, where Job says he "loathes" his life. It expresses a mixture of anger and grief. Perhaps the best word to describe it is "heartsick." That's what Jesus must have felt when He entered the Temple and found men buying and selling animals, and exchanging money. He fashioned a whip from cords, turned over heir tables and drove them out saying, "My house is a house of prayer and you have made it a den of thieves" (Luke 19:46).

The psalmist's feelings about his enemies were not based on their hate for him, but rather on their failure to respect and obey God's Word. They hated him because they hated his God and His Word.

Today, God's Word is widely ignored in our culture. Scholars attack its trustworthiness, and the movies and the media ridicule it. Its standards of moral behavior are ignored while evil is flaunted and pronounced to be good by the courts.

Do these things stir strong feelings within us? Do those of us who love God's Word feel a heartsickness akin to that of the psalmist? Are we grieved and angered when the Bible is trivialized, even in our churches?

I'm heartsick when I see
Those who disobey Thy Word,
As from Thy truth they flee
To the evil and absurd.

III. THE PSALMIST'S CONFIDENCE VS. 159-160

A. Based on God's Tender Ways v.159
Consider how I love Your precepts; Revive me O Lord, according to Your lovingkindness. In verse 54, the psalmist said, "Consider my affliction." Now he says, "Consider my affections." It's not how much we study God's Word, how much of it we can quote, how we can analyze it, but how much we love it. The psalmist loves God's Word because he loves God who spoke it. His Word leads to a deeper knowledge of the One who spoke the Word.

The Word tells him of God's tender mercies. He prays that God will revive him according to His lovingkindness. As we have noted before, lovingkindness is a covenant word rich in meaning for the Jewish people. It is expressed in God's goodwill toward His people. The psalmist is confident that it will not fail.

Thy precepts do I love.
They always make me wise
With wisdom from above
In answer to my cries.

277

B. Based on God's Truthful Word v.160
  1. It is entirely true v.160a
The entirety of Your word is true. The psalmist closes this stanza, as he has the last two, with an affirmation of the truth of God's Word. It's not part true and part error. It has been true from the beginning and it's still true. It has no half truths and it needs no updates.

Each precept, each ordinance, each judgment, and each decree is truth. What the Bible says about sin is true, no matter how many legislatures and courts may disagree. What it says about hell and the judgment is true, regardless of how few preachers declare it. What it says about salvation is true. What it declares about Jesus, who is the Truth, is true. Its prophecies and proverbs are equally true.

It is true regardless of what science says, regardless of what college professors say, or what the media say. It is true regardless of how many books are written to prove it wrong. Attacks upon it will not change its truth, nor will distortions of what it says. It will survive all challenges as it has always done.

Surveys show that most who claim to be born again don't believe in absolute truth. Yet God's Word is absolute truth whether we believe it or not. It's not, as someone has said, "God said it, I believe it, and that settles it." Rather, it is "God has said it, and that settles it."

  2. It is eternally true v.160b
And every one of Your righteous judgments endures forever. No matter how much the psalmist

suffered, he knew God's truth was unchanging. There is not, and never will be, any reason to amend God's Word. Generations may come and go, but God's Word stands forever. The psalmist found confidence and comfort in that knowledge. No matter how crazy our world gets, we too, can rest in the assurance that God's Word is truth we can trust forever.

Zemek said, "God's Book has proven itself to be both dependable and imperishable. For needy pilgrims it exudes its never-failing reliability which enables them, through a transcendent perspective, to endure and persevere amid the tempestuous tribulations of life in a hostile world,"

Somewhere there's a painting of an anvil with many broken hammers lying around it. Below the painting is the caption, "Hammer away ye hostile hands, your hammers break, God's anvil stands."

In Thy Word do I trust,
For it is holy and pure.
All its judgments are just,
And in them I am secure.

STANZA 21: PSALM 119:161-168

PEACE IN TIME OF AFFLICTION

I. A Persecuted Man vs.161-163
A. What He Felt v.161
B. What He Found v.162
C. What He Favored v.163
II. A Praising Man v.164
A. The Repetition of His Praise v.164a
B. The Reason for His Praise v.164b
III. A Peaceful Man vs. 165-168
A. His Outlook v.165
B. His Obedience v.166
C. His Overflowing v.167
D. His Openness v.168

As he nears the end of this great psalm, the psalmist takes on a different tone. There is no prayer in this stanza, only praise for God's Word. The psalmist speaks of his awe of it, his love for it, his joy in it, and affirms his obedience to it.

Spurgeon says of it, "We are drawing to the end. The pulse of the psalm beats more quietly than usual. The sentences are more full and deep. The veteran of a thousand battles, the receiver of a thousand mercies, rehearses his experiences and declares anew his loyalty to the Lord and His law."

I. A PERSECUTED MAN VS.161-163

A. What He Felt v.161

Princes persecute me without a cause. But my heart stands in awe of Your word. In verse 23, the psalmist says that princes speak against him, now they persecute him. We would expect the authorities of the world, who are appointed by God to do good and administer justice (Rom.13:1-4), to protect rather than persecute the children of God. But the psalmist didn't find it so, nor have multitudes of believers since. In many cases the civil authorities, who we expect to do good, do evil to those who are trying to do good.

However, the psalmist's persecutors didn't persecute him for what he had done, but rather for who he was. They needed no other reason. The persecutors of the righteous are subject to the god of this world. Their position of authority does not change their hearts. It only gives them the power to perform their evil deeds.

In Psalm 35:7, David wrote, "For without cause they have hidden their net for me in a pit, which they have dug without cause for my life." He also said in Psalm 69:4, "Those who hate me without a cause are more than the hairs of my head. They are mighty who would destroy me." Jesus tried to get His enemies to identify a reason for their desire to kill Him. "Many good works I have shown you from My Father. For which of these works do you stone me" (John 10:32-33)?

David was pursued and persecuted by Saul without a cause (I Sam.19:5). Daniel was thrown to the lions for no good reason. The three Hebrew companions of Daniel were thrown into the firey furnace without cause. According to tradition, all the apostles, except John, were killed by the authorities. Their only crime was preaching the gospel.

What do Christians do today to deserve persecution and ridicule? They minister to the sick, feed the poor, educate the ignorant and proclaim the good news of the forgiveness of sins. For these things they are scorned, and sometimes imprisoned, even killed.

However, persecution by princes didn't distract the psalmist from his reverence for God's Word. The word translated "awe" is used only three times in the Old Testament. In Psalm 4:4 and Psalm 33:8, it refers to God. Here, it refers to His Word. So, only God and His Word are referred to as awesome in the Bible.

God looks with favor upon those who reverence His Word. "But upon this one will I look, upon him who is poor and of a contrite spirit, and who trembles at My word" (Isa. 66:2). Matthew Henry said, "They that tremble at the conviction of the Word may triumph in the consolation of it" (Matthew Henry's Commentary). This is what the psalmist did.

> Pursued by those who hate,
> Yet to Thy Word I hold,
> And upon Thee I'll wait
> Until the end be told.

B. What He Found v.162

I rejoice at Your word as one who finds great treasure. The KJV says, "as one who finds great spoil." This is probably what is meant here. In ancient times, after a battle the victorious army took the goods of the defeated army as the spoils of battle. Sometimes the spoils were won after great effort. Sometimes the armies that fought against Israel were defeated by the hand of God with no effort required by Israel.

We have such a case in II Chronicles 20 when the armies of Ammon, Moab, and Mt. Seir came against King Jehoshaphat of Judah. Jehoshaphat called for a prayer meeting in Jerusalem, and then sent the choir out in advance of the Army. As Israel watched, the Lord confused the invading armies so that they fought against one another. After they destroyed one another, it took Israel three days to gather the spoils.

The psalmist has already referred to the Word being more valuable to him than gold and silver (v.72). Now, it brings him joy like the joy of taking great spoil in battle. This suggests that his joy in God's Word came because of his great affliction and the suffering he had endured at the hands of his enemies. God's Word has been his constant companion and comfort through many battles. Now it's his most precious treasure.

Of all the spoils of earth,
Thy Word is the greatest of all.
It is of unmeasured worth
To those who upon Thee shall call.

C. What He Favored v.163

I hate and abhor lying, but I love Your law. In verses 29-30, the psalmist asks the Lord to remove from him the way of lying because he had chosen the way of truth. Now he says he hates and abhors lying.

One can't love lying and love God's Word. He has already declared God's Word to be entirely and forever true (v.160). His love for the law is as intense as his hatred of lying. What we love determines what we hate. Psalm 97:10 says, "You who love the Lord, hate evil!" God is totally opposed to any untruth, and love for God and His word can't co-exist with love for lying.

Satan is a liar and the father of lies. He would have us believe there is no real truth. The battle between truth and lies started in the Garden of Eden when Satan cast doubt on the truth of what God had said. The devil is still casting doubt on God's Word. The lines between truth and lies are so blurred today that even the church no longer declares the truth with a clear voice. Our culture is very tolerant of various shades of lying.

The person who can say with the psalmist, "I hate and abhor lying, but I love Your law," is rare

today. These words are seldom heard today from our
pulpits.

> All lying Lord, I detest,
> But Thy law do I love,
> And I will make it my quest,
> For it's truth from above.

II. THE PRAISING MAN V.164

A. The Repetition of His Praise v.164a

Seven times a day I praise You. Seven is the divine
number, the number of perfection. The frequency
of the psalmist's praise was not based on any legal
requirement or established custom. There was no
rule that compelled him to bow seven times a day at
an appointed time, as with Muslims who bow toward
Mecca five times a day. Rather, it was the spontaneous impulse of a heart full of praise.

Praise was an antidote for the persecution he had
endured at the hands of his enemies. Every word of
praise was another log on the fire of love that burned
in his heart. Nothing can take away our ability to
praise God. We can praise Him anywhere at any time.
I remember a dying man in a retirement home who
was in great pain. He couldn't attend the services we
conducted in the lobby, but we could hear his shouts
of praise from his room.

B. The Reasons for His Praise v.164b

...because of Your Righteous judgments. His
reasons for praise were based on God's righteous

judgments which are recorded in His Word. Every day he found new reasons for praise in God's Word, sometimes in the stories of God's mighty deeds, sometimes in His promises, and sometimes in the commandments that guided his steps.

Surely, we too, can find reasons to praise God every day. However, we must ask with Spurgeon, "Do we praise Him seven times a day, or do we praise Him once in seven days?" Even in our darkest days we can find reasons to praise Him.

> Seven times a day I pause
> To lift my heart in praise,
> For the greatness of Thy laws,
> Which guide me in Thy ways.

III. THE PEACEFUL MAN VS.165-168

A. His Outlook v.165

Great peace have they who love Your law, and nothing causes them to stumble. The psalmist has a positive outlook because he knows from studying the law that God is in control and all things will work according to His plan. It gives him calmness in the face of difficulty.

The peace here is not the peace with God that comes from forgiveness and reconciliation with God through Christ. It's the peace of God which Christ speaks of in John 16:33, "These things I have spoken unto you that in Me you may have peace. In the world you will have tribulation, but I have overcome the world."

This peace is not given to those who know the law best, but to those who love it most, and are devoted to obeying it. Loving the Word focuses our attention on Him who spoke the Word. Isaiah said, "He will keep him in perfect peace whose mind is stayed on You, because he trusts in You" (Isa. 26:3)

Those who love the Word are anchored to it and can survive the fiercest storms. In times of trouble they cling to it. When they are tempted, it is their defense. They do not stumble and fall into the pits of despair. They are not tripped up by the devil's traps, nor yield to the pressure of their peers.

> They who love Thy law have peace,
> And nothing shall cause them to fall,
> For Thy Word shall never cease,
> And in it is no error at all.

B. His Obedience v.166

Lord, I hope for Your salvation, and I do Your commandments. As explained elsewhere, the word "hope" expresses more than a vague wish. It means a strong inner confidence and assurance. It's the basis of our faith. "Faith is the substance of things hoped for" (Heb.11:1).

As we have noted before, the salvation referred to in the Old Testament was deliverance from any present or future danger. Its meaning is not limited to the New Testament doctrine of deliverance from sin through Christ.

In this verse, we have the two legs of the holy life – placing our hope in the Lord and keeping His commandments. It's the message of the old hymn, "Trust and Obey." It's expressed in the New Testament in Ephesians 2:8-9, where Paul tells us that we are saved by grace through faith, but we are saved unto good works. Our hope is not in the good works, but in the Lord. However, those who hope in the Lord for salvation will keep His commandments.

The psalmist has not just read the commandments, he has obeyed them. By obedience his hope is strengthened. His obedience doesn't mean he is perfect, but it is a lifestyle he passionately pursues. In the previous verse, he declared his love for the law. Now he obeys it, as do all who love it.

In Thee O Lord, I trust
And seek Thy Word to obey,
For all Thy laws are just,
And righteous is Thy way.

C. His Overflowing v.167

My soul keeps Your testimonies, and I love them exceedingly. We can feel the psalmist's intensity building. His sentences are growing shorter and his words sharper. First, he speaks of the peace of those who love God's law (v.165). Now he says he loves it exceedingly. In verse 166, he speaks of doing God's commandments. Now he declares that his soul keeps them. The expression "my soul" is used throughout the psalms to express deep feelings. So he is saying that he keeps God's testimonies with deep emotion. Soul obedience is emotional obedience, as opposed to grudging obedience motivated by duty.

Emotion without action is meaningless, and action without emotion is lifeless. When our feelings and actions are linked together, it's pleasing to the Lord and a delight to us. We find pleasure in doing what we love to do. The more we feed on God's Word and obey it, the more we love it. The more we love it, the more we delight in obeying it. It's the golden circle of a happy life.

I love Thy Word without measure.
My passion for it is intense.
I obey it with great pleasure,
For in it I find no offense.

D. His Openness v. 168

I keep Your percepts and Your testimonies, For all my ways are open before You. The theme of obedience, so prominent in the last two verses, continues in this one. In the previous verse, the psalmist implies that his obedience is driven by his exceeding love for God's testimonies. In this verse, it's because his ways are open before the Lord.

In Job 34:21, Elihu said, "For all His eyes are on the ways of man, and He sees all his ways." Solomon said, "For the ways of man are before the Lord, and He ponders all his paths" (Prov.5:21). In the New Testament, the writer of Hebrews tells us, "And there is no creature hidden from His sight, but all things are naked and open to the eyes of Him with whom we have to do" (Heb.4:13).

Whether the all-seeing eye of God comforts or condemns us depends on whether or not we keep

His precepts. The Openness of our ways to God is a terrifying fact to those who walk in darkness, but is a blessed comfort to those who walk in the light. For the psalmist, it was a powerful reason for obedience. It appears that he may have been calling on the omniscient God to witness the truth of what he had just declared.

We may hide God from our eyes, but we can never hide ourselves from His. Let us open our hearts to Him and pray with David, "Search me, O God, and know my heart. Try me and know my anxieties; and see if there is any wicked way in me, and lead me in the way everlasting" (Ps.51:23-24).

Before Thee the darkness flees,
As Thine eye pierces the night.
So I fall upon my knees
And seek to walk in Thy light.

THE
PSALMIST'S
LAST PLEA

I. He Pleads for a Heavenly Hearing vs.169-172
    A. His Petitions vs.169-170
        1. For discernment v.169
        2. For deliverance v.170
    B. His Promises vs.171-172
        1. To praise God's ways v.171
        2. To proclaim God's Word v.172
II. He Pleads for a Helping Hand vs.173-176
    A. To Save Him vs.173-174
        1. His decision v.173
        2. His desires v.174
    B. To Sustain Him v.175
        1. With inspiration v.175a
        2. With instruction v.175b
    C. To Seek Him v.176

1. The straying sheep v.176a
2. The seeking shepherd v.176b

We have walked with the psalmist through 21 stanzas of this great psalm. We have shared his deep love for God's Word and for the God who spoke it. Now he sums it all up and makes a final plea.

Spurgeon said, "His petitions gather still more force and fervency. He seems to break into the inner circle of divine fellowship, and come to the feet of the great God whose help he is imploring. This nearness creates the most lowly view of himself, and leads him to close the psalm prostrate in the dust, in deep self-humiliation, begging to be sought like a sheep."

The psalmist introduces five of his petitions in this stanza with the word "let," symbolizing his humility and unworthiness. He presents his petitions in the form of a plea, not a demand.

I. HE PLEADS FOR A HEAVENLY HEARING VS.169-172

A. His Petitions vs.169-170
1. For discernment v.169
Let my cry come before You O Lord, Give me understanding according to Your word. The psalmist's petition is in the form of the cry of a child to its father. He wants God to hear the cry of his heart, not just the sound of his voice. It's not the eloquence of

our words, but the cry of our hearts that get the attention of our heavenly Father.

His cry is for understanding. He has prayed for understanding before, and claimed to have it more than his teachers (vs.34,75,99,141). His repetition of this request indicates the earnestness of his desire.

Understanding comes only from God. "There is a spirit in man and the breath of the Almighty gives him understanding" (Job 32:8). Paul prayed that the Lord would give Timothy "understanding in all things" (II Tim. 2:7). All discernment given by God is in accord with His Word.

> Lord, incline to me Thine ear
> And let my cry be heard.
> May Thy truth to me be clear
> According to Thy Word.

2. For deliverance v.170

Let my supplication come before You, deliver me according to Your word. He makes the same humble plea as in verse 169, changing the word "cry" to "supplication." It's a beggar's petition, and he is seeking an audience with God to present it. The word translated "supplication" involves the idea of granting favor in the submission of a petition or prayer.

Throughout the psalm, the psalmist has been persecuted, afflicted, slandered and oppressed. Now he makes a final plea for deliverance from his enemies who have tormented him. The discernment he asked for in verse 169 may be the deliverance he is asking for in this verse. Sometimes we find deliverance from perplexing situations through greater insight and understanding.

> Let my prayers come to Thee
> And grant to me Thy favor.
> May Thy hand deliver me
> And my heart never waiver.

B. His Promises vs.171-172
  1. To praise God's ways v.171

My lips shall utter praise, for You teach me Your statutes. He prayed for discernment and deliverance. Both are reasons for praise. The word translated "utter" is *naba* which means to bubble up, to gush out or belch forth. The idea is that a spontaneous outpouring of praise gushes from his lips.

The praises he utters are deeply rooted in the Word of God. True praise is based on knowledge of God's Word. Empty headed praise is no praise at all. Some of today's praise music repeat "praise God," over and over again without ever giving any reason for the praise. Someone has called it "7-11" music, which is 7 words repeated 11 times. Only heavenly knowledge can produce heavenly praise.

The more we learn of Him the more reason we have to praise Him. The psalmist had far less of the written Word of God than we do, yet he found many reasons to praise Him. Today we have the complete Scriptures and a much greater understanding of God's purpose. How much greater are our reasons for praising God!

As our knowledge increases from the study of the Bible, our praise should increase. When we finally throw off this earthly tabernacle and enter the place Christ has prepared for us, our praises will continue to increase and fill heaven because our knowledge will be complete.

> Lord, I lift my voice in praise
> For all Thy hand has brought,
> And the knowledge of Thy ways,
> Which to us Thou hast taught.

2. To proclaim God's Word v.172

My tongue shall speak of Your word, for all Your commandments are righteous. Spurgeon said, "When he is done singing he began preaching. God's tender mercies are such that they can be either said, or sung." So there is first praise, then proclamation.

The psalmist has been taught and now he becomes a teacher. Having learned that God's commandments are the righteous standard by which all righteousness is measured, he can't keep silent. First, he bubbles over with praise, then he breaks forth in preaching. When he speaks God's Word he will never be in error for it is the essence of truth. Not only is God's Word true in general, but every one of His commandments are righteous.

Too often we are full of our own words, but speak so little of God's words. Very few of our words are worth hearing once, and most are never worth repeating. But all God's words are full of inexhaustible wisdom which grows wider and deeper with each repetition.

> In my heart Thy words do burn,
> So let my tongue proclaim
> Thy truth that others may learn
> The greatness of Thy name!

II. HE PLEADS FOR A HELPING HAND
VS.173-176

A. To Save Him vs.173-174

1. His decision v.173

Let Your hand become my help, for I have chosen Your precepts. Again, the psalmist makes his supplication introduced by the word "let" This time he pleads for God to reach out His hand and help him, although he doesn't say what kind of help he needs. God's hand is a symbol of God's work. He wants God to work on his behalf. In God's hand is the power and skill to meet any need.

The psalmist's plea for help is based on his decision to live by God's precepts. We may appropriately expect help from God when we commit ourselves to obey His Word. "Give us help from trouble. For the help of men is useless. Through God we will do valiantly, for it is He who shall tread down our enemies" (Ps.60:11-12).

God promises to help His people. "Fear not, I will be with you. Be not dismayed for I am your God. I will strengthen you. Yea, I will help you. I will uphold you with My righteous hand" (Isa. 41:10).

Often we are like Paul who cried, "To will is present in me, but how to perform what is good, I do not find" (Rom.5:18). In such times we need God's help.

Life is a series of choices, and choices have consequences. When we, like the psalmist, decide to live by the Word of God, we can expect God to help us do it. If we decide to disobey, we must live with the results of our decision.

Lay bare O Lord, Thy hand.
O help; me in my need,
For on Thy Word I stand
And follow Thee indeed!

2. His desire v.174

I long for Your salvation, O Lord, and Your law is my delight. The first phrase tells us what the psalmist desires. The second tells us what delights him. What we desire depends on what delights us. To put it another way, what we long for is based on what we love.

The psalmist longs for God's salvation, or deliverance. He doesn't just long for any deliverance, but for God's deliverance. We can't depend on the deliverances that the world offers. Science offers to save us; government promises to save us from various discomforts and inconveniences; education claims it will save us from ignorance, and give us a better life. However, few seek the salvation that God promises to those who trust Him.

Again, the psalmist doesn't give us any detail about what he longs to be delivered from. Perhaps he is longing for God to deliver him from the trials of this life as well as sin and judgment through the coming Savior.

In Thy Word I find delight,
And Thy salvation my desire.
So reveal to me Thy light,
And may my heart be set on fire.

B. To Sustain Him v.175
 1. With inspiration v.175a

Let my soul live and it shall praise You. The psalmist has often prayed for revival in the midst of his affliction. Trouble drains our strength from us. He needed new inspiration to continue. That's what he is praying for here. "Though I walk in the midst of trouble, You will revive me; You will stretch out Your hand against the wrath of my enemies, and Your right hand will save me" (Ps.138:7).

He needs the vitality to praise God. He wants to be preserved from dryness and deadness. Inspired living requires a touch from God.

 2. With instruction v.175b

...And let Your judgments help me. In verse 173, he said, "Let Your hand become my help." Here he prays for God's judgments to help him. He is asking for instruction and insight from reading the record of God's acts and declarations in God's Word. So, in this verse, he is asking God to revive him by the Spirit and instruct him from the Word. Life comes

from the Spirit and light from the Word. That's all we need today!

> O Lord, let me live.
> I pray my soul to inspire
> That I may to Thee give
> All the praise that I desire.

C. To Seek Him v.176
1. The straying sheep v.176a
I have gone astray like a lost sheep. After 22 stanzas and 175 verses of prayers, praises, meditation and affirmations of his love for God's Word, the psalmist confesses that he is still like a lost and straying sheep. The tendency to stray never ends, no matter how steadfast our resolves and how passionate our desires to obey.

The psalmist has often defended himself against his enemies and his oppressors. However, when he comes before the Lord, he confesses that he is like a straying sheep who has wandered away from the fold and the shepherd.

2. The seeking shepherd v.176b
Seek Your servant for I do not forget Your commandments. He is like a straying sheep, yet he is also the Lord's servant who wants to be found and restored to his master's house.

Dogs may wander from home, but usually find their way back. A sheep can get lost between the barn and the haystack, and will wander farther away unless it is found and brought back.

The psalmist bases his request to be brought back on the fact that he has not forgotten the Lord's commandments. It's a good argument. One who remembers the precepts and longs for them is not satisfied to continue straying from them. Just as the prodigal son never forgot his father's house, the saint, with the Word in his heart, has a continual longing for fellowship with the Father. Straying doesn't erase the Word from our hearts. It only makes us dissatisfied with our straying.

For those sheep who do not yet belong to the Father, His message to them is found in Isaiah 53:6, "All we like sheep have gone astray. We have turned every one to his own way, but the Lord has laid upon Him (Jesus) the iniquity of us all." Those who accept Jesus as their sin bearer become the sheep of the father's fold.

O Lord, I'm prone to wander.
Let me not go astray,
For in my heart I ponder
All Thy Word to obey.

APPENDIX

HOW TO GET THE MOST FROM YOUR BIBLE READING
By Thomas Watson (1620-1686)

(Provided by Fire and Ice: Puritan and Reformed Writings)

1. Remove hindrances. (a) Remove the love of every sin. (b) Remove the distracting concerns of this world, especially covetousness (Matt. 13:22). (c) Don't make jokes with and out of Scripture.
2. Prepare your heart (I Sam.7:3). Do this by (a) collecting your thoughts (b) purging unclean affections and desires (c) not coming to it rashly or carelessly.
3. Read it with reverence, considering that each line is God speaking directly to you.
4. Read the books of the Bible in order.

5. Get a true understanding of Scripture (Ps.110:33). This is best achieved by comparing relevant parts of Scripture with each other.

6. Read with seriousness Deut. 32:47). The Christian life is to be taken seriously, since it requires striving and not falling short (Heb. 4:1).

7. Persevere in remembering what you read (Ps. 119:15). Don't let it be stolen from you (Matt. 13:4,19). If it does not stay in your memory it is unlikely to be much benefit to you.

8. Meditate on what you read ((Ps. 119:52). The Hebrew word for meditate means to be intense in your mind. Meditation without reading is sure to err; reading without meditation is barren and fruitless. It means to stir the affections, to be warmed by the fire of meditation (Ps. 39:3).

9. Read with a humble heart. Acknowledge that you are unworthy that God should reveal Himself to you (James 4:6).

10. Believe it all to be God's holy Word (II Tim. 3:18). We know that no sinner could have written it because of the way it describes sin. No saint could blaspheme God by pretending his own word was God's. No angel could have written it for the same reason (Heb. 4:2).

11. Prize the Bible highly (Ps. 119:72). It is your life-line. You were born by it (James 1:18), you grow by it (I Peter 2:2) cf. Job 23:12.

12. Love the Bible ardently (Ps. 119:150).

13. Come to read it with an honest heart (Luke 8:15), (a) willing to know the entire and complete will

of God, (b) reading in order to be changed and made better (John 17:17).

14. Apply to yourself everything you read. Take every word as spoken to yourself; its condemnation of sins as your own sin; at he duty that it requires as the duty God would require from you (II Kings 22:11).

15. Pay close attention to the commands of the Word as much as the promises. Think of how you need direction just as much as you need comfort.

16. Don't get carried away with the minor details, rather make sure to pay closest attention to the great things (Hosea 8:12).

17. Compare yourself with the Word. How do you compare? Is your heart something of a transcript of it or not?

18. Pay special attention to those passages that speak to your individual, particular situation.

19. Pay special attention to the examples and lives of people in the Bible as living sermons. (a) Punishments (Nebuchadnezzar, Herod etc.) Num.25:3-4 & 9, I Kings 14:9-10, Acts 5:5,10, I Cor. 10:11, Jude 7. (b) Mercies and deliverances (Daniel, Jeremiah, the three youths in the firey furnace).

20. Don't stop reading the Bible until you find your heart warmed (Ps.119:93). Let it not only inform you, but inflame you (Jer. 23:29, Luke 24:32).

21. Put into practice what you read (Ps. 119:66, 105, Deut. 17:19).

22. Christ is for us Prophet, Priest and King. Make use of His office as prophet (Rev. 5:5, John 8:6,

Ps. 119:102-103). Get Christ not only to open the Scriptures up to you, but to open your mind and understanding (Luke 24:45).

23. Make sure to put yourself under a true ministry of the Word, faithfully expounding the Word (Prov.8:34). Be earnest and eager in waiting on it.

24. Pray that you will profit from reading (Isa. 48:14, Ps. 119:18, Neh. 9:20).

Your may still be able to profit from reading the Word even though:

1. You don't seem to profit as much as other do. Remember the different yields (Matt. 13:8). Though the yield isn't as much as others, it is still a true yield.

2. You may feel slow of understanding (Luke 9:45, Heb. 5:11).

3. Your memory is bad. (a) Remember you are still able to have a good heart despite this. (b) You may still remember the most important things even if you cannot remember everything. Be encouraged by John 14:26.

OTHER RESOURCES

Adams, Jeff. *Psalm 119,* Reality Living Publishers, Kansas City, MO 1993

Boice, James Montgomery. *Living by the Book,* Baker Books, Grand Rapids, MI 1997

Bridges, Charles. *Psalm 119, An Exposition,* Banner of Truth Trust, Carlisle, PA 1974

Fearey, Marcy. *The Word Magnified,* Revival Nation Publishing, Sarina, Ontario, 2008

Hocking, David. *Psalm 119,* Biola University, La Mirada, CA 1989

Kneip, Seth. *Loving God's Word,* Lifesong Publishing, Somas, CA 2007

Logsdon, Franklin. *The Victory Life in Psalm 119,* Moody Press, Chicago, IL 1960

Manton, Thomas. *Psalm 119, 3 Volumes,* Banner of Truth Trust, Carlisle, PA 1990

Phillips, John. *Exploring the Psalms Vol. 2,* Loizeaux Brothers, Neptune, NJ 1988

Spurgeon, Charles. *The Golden Alphabet*, Pilgrim Publications, Pasadena, TX 1980

Spurgeon, Charles. *The Treasury of David Vol. 3,* Hendrickson Publishers, Peabody, MA 1982

Zemik, George J. *The Word of God in the Child of God,* Privately published.